Annuals

BY THE EDITORS OF SUNSET BOOKS AND SUNSET MAGAZINE

Planted in profusion, summer annuals dress up entry steps,
offering a colorful welcome.

Sunset Publishing Corporation ■ Menlo Park, California

Pansy (Viola wittrockiana) 'Jolly Joker'

Research & Text
Lance Walheim

Contributing Editor
Mary E. Harrison

Coordinating Editor
Linda J. Selden

Design
Joe di Chiarro

Illustrations
Lois Lovejoy
Jane McCreary

Calligraphy
Sherry Bringham

Editor, Sunset Books: Elizabeth L. Hogan

First printing January 1992

Photographers

Scott Atkinson: 36, 38, 41, 42, 45; **Liz Ball/Photo/Nats:** 50 top, 51 top; **Glenn Christiansen:** 7; **Priscilla Connell/Photo/Nats:** 50 top middle, 62 bottom; **John R. Dunmire:** 67 top left; **Thomas E. Eltzroth:** 29 top, 55 top right, 61 bottom, 62 top left, 74 bottom, 81 top right, 88 top left; **Derek Fell:** 51 bottom middle, 51 bottom, 54 left, 58 left, 59 right, 62 top right, 64 top, 76 top left and bottom, 85 left, 92 top right; **Saxon Holt:** 2, 4, 8, 10, 11, 12, 15, 16, 17, 18, 19, 20, 21, 22 right, 23 bottom right, 24, 29 bottom, 30 left, 31, 32 bottom, 33 bottom, 34, 35, 39, 52, 54 right, 55 top left and bottom, 58 right, 59 middle, 60 top right and bottom, 63 top, 64 bottom, 65, 66, 67 top right and bottom, 68 top right and bottom, 69, 70 top and middle, 71, 72 bottom, 74 top left, 75 left, 77, 78 top right and bottom, 79, 80 top right and bottom, 81 top left, 82 middle, 83, 85 right, 86, 87 top left, 88 bottom left, 90, 91 top, 92 top left, 94 top; **Horticultural Photography:** 27 bottom, 57, 61 top, 73 bottom, 75 right, 78 top left, 81 bottom, 82 top, 84 top left and right, 87 bottom, 88 top right, 89 bottom; **Robert E. Lyons/Photo/Nats:** 51 middle; **Ells Marugg:** 56 bottom; **Robert and Linda Mitchell:** 50 bottom middle, 51 top middle, 87 top right; **Norman A. Plate:** 1, 25, 40, 59 left, 63 bottom; **Bill Ross:** 14, 23 top and bottom left, 25 top, 26 left, 27 top, 72 top left, 80 top left, 88 bottom right, 94 bottom; **Teri Sandison:** 72 top right; **David M. Stone/Photo/Nats:** 91 bottom; **David Stubbs:** 50 bottom; **Michael S. Thompson:** 22 left, 30 right, 32 top, 56 top left, 60 top left, 68 top left, 73 top, 76 top right, 89 top, 92 bottom left, 93 top left and bottom; **Darrow M. Watt:** 28, 33 top, 56 top right, 70 bottom, 74 top right, 82 bottom, 84 bottom, 93 top right; **Russ A. Widstrand:** 26 right.

Gardening with Color

Flowering annuals are extremely rewarding plants to grow. They can turn your garden into a vibrant tapestry of color or, used with restraint, provide just enough accent to make everything else in your landscape look fresher and more interesting.

But using annuals successfully takes thoughtful planning. This book will show you how to mix and match colors, how to achieve the longest possible season of bloom, and how to select just the right annuals for particular planting sites. We also explain how to care for annuals—from seed to transplant to full bloom.

As a group, flowering annuals comprise an amazingly diverse group of plants. To help you explore this diversity, we describe more than 100 species in the last chapter, Annuals A to Z.

For carefully checking our manuscript, special thanks go to Tilly Holtrop of Goldsmith Seeds, Gilroy, California; Roslyn Doss of Park Seed Company, Greenwood, South Carolina; and Jim Nau of Ball Seed Company, West Chicago, Illinois. We'd also like to extend thanks to Nona E. Wolfram-Koivula of All-America Selections, Downers Grove, Illinois and Burlingame Garden Center. Finally, we thank Marcia Williamson for her careful editing of the manuscript.

$\mathscr{C}$ontents

Viola

The Versatile Annuals 5
More Than Just Colorful Flowers

Annuals in the Garden 9
Gardening with Color

How to Grow Annuals 37
Care from Seed to Bloom

Annuals A to Z 53
Abelmoschus to Zinnia

Index 95

Special Features

Average Hard-Frost Dates **39**

Starting from Seed **43**

A Fertilizer Primer **47**

Container Gardening **49**

Seed Sources **94**

The Versatile Annuals

*G*arden color is what most people expect from flowering annuals. And it's true: no other group of plants can so quickly create a tapestry of bold or subtle colors, and at so little expense. Annuals are garden color, in every hue and tone imaginable. But besides being colorful, annuals are also versatile. They represent a huge, incredibly diverse class of plants that can play a variety of roles in the garden.

Cosmos

Lobelia, phlox, salvia, and sweet alyssum (Lobularia) yield a stunning combination of annual color and texture.

What Is an Annual?

Botanically, an annual is a plant that completes its life cycle in a year or less. The seed germinates, the plant grows, flowers, sets new seed, and dies—all in one growing season. The seeds set by many annuals will fall to the ground and, conditions permitting, germinate at some time in the future, usually the following winter or spring. These volunteers, as they are often called, can be left in place to flower, but they are likely to differ in habit or flower color from their parents.

Annuals are usually compared to perennials, which are defined as nonwoody plants that live for more than two years. Depending on how well they are adapted to where they are being grown, perennials can usually be counted on to bloom year after year, with bloom improving as plants mature.

Between annuals and perennials are biennials, which complete their life cycle in two years. The first year, they develop foliage; the second year, they bloom, set seed, and die.

Even though in a botanical sense annuals, perennials, and biennials fit into neatly defined categories, the distinctions that separate them are often blurred in nurseries and home gardens. Many tender perennials (such as geraniums, primroses, and verbenas), which will bloom year after year in mild-winter climates, are treated like annuals where winters are cold. Because they are quick to bloom, they can also be treated like annuals in mild-winter areas. In other words, even though they might bloom again the next year, the plants are discarded at the end of the season to make room for others. (In that sense, any plant that blooms within a year after you buy it could be considered an annual.)

Some biennials, including hollyhocks and Canterbury bells, can also be treated like annuals. If you buy nursery transplants and set them out early enough, they will bloom the first season. In essence, the nurseryman has provided the first growing season.

Cool-season Annuals Versus Warm-season Annuals

Annuals can be considered cool-season or warm-season plants, depending on their hardiness and ability to grow in cool soils.

Cool-season annuals (such as pansies, primroses, and calendulas) usually do best in the cool soils and mild temperatures of fall and spring. They are hardy to varying degrees (some are technically perennials), with most withstanding fairly heavy frosts. With the onset of hot weather, cool-season annuals are usually quick to set seed and deteriorate. In areas with short or cool summers, many cool-season annuals perform well all summer long. In addition, some varieties have been bred for greater heat tolerance and can bloom longer into warm weather. Where winters are mild, many cool-season annuals can be planted in fall for winter and early-spring bloom.

Warm-season annuals (such as marigolds, zinnias, and impatiens) grow and flower best in the warm months of late spring, summer, and early fall. Since most are sensitive to frost, they are planted after the average date of the last spring frost. Their bloom season usually ends with the first frost of fall.

Varieties, Hybrids & Strains

Seed companies, plant breeders, and growers have gone to great lengths to provide the highest-quality flowering annuals. Through careful breeding and vigilant selection of superior types, annuals are constantly being improved. These improvements include more and earlier bloom, wider color range, improved plant habit and vigor, and resistance to disease and insects.

The results of these improvements are offered to you as named varieties, such as 'Apricot Brandy' celosia or 'Royal Carpet' alyssum. Annual varieties are usually F-1 hybrids, which means they result from the cross-pollination of two specific plants, and are designated with single quotes. This pollination usually takes place under controlled conditions, such as in a greenhouse, so the results are uniform.

Some annual seed is produced through open pollination, meaning that the parent plants are grown in fields and the flowers are pollinated naturally, by wind or insects. Since you can never be sure exactly which plants were the parents, there is always a chance for variability among annuals grown from seed produced by open-pollinated plants. However, many open-pollinated plants do come "true to type," meaning that seeds grown from them will result in plants that are identical or very similar to the source of the seed. A strain, such as State Fair zinnias, is a group of plants that share similar growth characteristics but are variable in some one respect, usually flower color.

If you decide to save seeds or let your annuals reseed themselves, you need to be aware of another important distinction between F-1 hybrids and open-pollinated varieties. Seed collected from F-1 hybrids is not likely to produce plants identical to the parents. Unless pollination is controlled, the next generation will probably be significantly different in flower or plant form. Seed collected from open-pollinated plants is more likely to resemble parent plants.

All-America Selections

Each year the All-America Selection (AAS) organization judges new annual and vegetable varieties for exceptional performance. Nearly 100 varieties are planted at more than 50 trial gardens throughout the United States and Canada. Each annual is evaluated by impartial experts for its overall garden merit, local adaptation, length of bloom season, and vigor. On average, four varieties are given medals as outstanding performers. You'll find AAS award winners called out in many seed catalogs, in nurseries, and in the "Annuals A to Z" section of this book (pages 53 to 94). These plants can be counted on for superior bloom or outstanding garden performance.

Using This Book

Begin your experience with flowering annuals with an understanding of how to use them in the garden. "Designing with Annuals," starting on page 10, gives basic suggestions on how to combine and contrast colors and plant textures. The seasonal color charts help you plan for the longest possible period of bloom. Lists of annuals for specific growing conditions (such as for sun or shade) and with particular growth habits (such as low-growing or tall) help you select plants that fit your garden conditions and landscape needs. And lists of annuals with special characteristics (such as distinctive flower fragrance) encourage you to fashion a colorful landscape that expresses your own personal style.

The chapter "How to Grow Annuals," beginning on page 37, provides all the basics on culture: choosing a planting site, preparing the soil, germinating seed, growing healthy transplants, providing adequate water and nutrients, and controlling pests.

But the heart and soul of this book begin on page 53, where the plant encyclopedia opens. There you'll find full descriptions of more than 100 annuals, with all the information you'll need to successfully grow each one.

An artistically designed planting of annuals, including calendulas, zinnias, larkspur (Consolida), nigella, and hollyhocks (Alcea), creates a meadow of casual-looking color.

Annuals in the Garden

lowering annuals are the workhorses of the flower garden. No other single group of plants can, in such a short time, so dramatically affect how a garden looks and feels. Flowering annuals can create interest in a dull green landscape or spotlight the best features of an exciting one. They can make a garden seem more relaxing or a front entry more inviting. They stimulate the senses, directing the eye from place to place, or making a cool spot seem warmer or a hot one more comfortable and appealing.

Antirrhinum majus

Annuals splash a riot of color across what was once a green garden. The boldly colored flowers include marigolds (Tagetes), salvia, petunias, and phlox.

9

Designing with Annuals

A well-timed mixture of cool-season annuals contrasts rich-toned snapdragons (Antirrhinum) with cool whites of sweet alyssum (Lobularia) and chrysanthemums.

The impact of annuals has much to do with their vibrant colors. But the most effective plantings are more than eye-catching splashes of color. They make use of texture, plant habit, and flower form, and rely on subtle complements and contrasts to create a specific look or mood.

Success depends to a certain extent on experience. But if you're new to gardening with annuals, you can still expect many more pleasant surprises than disappointments. Plant choices are many, and expanding every year; there is always something new. As you explore the possibilities, try keeping a garden journal to record varieties and flower combinations you especially liked, and to note where they were planted and when they bloomed. You'll soon build your own fund of knowledge with which to ensure future success.

Following a few simple guidelines will help you use flowering annuals most effectively.

Timing. When a plant flowers depends on many things, including the nature of the plant itself (see pages 53 to 94), your local climate, the planting site, and the weather. Some of these factors you can't control, and some you can. Still, annuals are usually grouped by the season in which they flower: spring, summer, fall, or, in mild-winter areas, winter. And that is the best place to start when planning a flower garden. But if you want to establish a long period of color, it's also important to think about how your garden will swing from one season to the next.

When spring annuals finish flowering, will you pull them all out and replant with new summer annuals, leaving several weeks when nothing will be in bloom? Or will you gradually work young summer annuals in among the flowering spring annuals so they'll be coming into bloom as the others finish? How will that affect your color scheme? What about planting spring- and summer-flowering annuals in separate places?

There are many ways to keep a garden in bloom month after month. You can purchase blooming plants in 4-inch pots or gallon cans so seasonal changes are barely noticeable. You can also plant young annuals in containers and keep them in a staging area until they are looking their best.

The important thing is to have a well-thought-out plan, especially if you'll be buying seeds and starting them yourself. Remember, if you want pansies in bloom in April, you may have to order seed 3 months in advance and sow it 8 to 10 weeks before transplant time.

Matching cultural needs. Some annuals grow best in sun, some in shade. Some bloom vigorously with constant moisture, and others take to soil on the dry side. Some annuals respond to regular fertilizer applications, and others will not bloom if the soil is too rich in nitrogen.

It's easiest to meet cultural needs by planting a bed with one type of annual. If you are mixing different plants, make sure they have similar cultural requirements.

Staggering heights. Keep the short plants in front and the taller ones toward the back. If you put the tall plants in front, you won't be able to see the smaller ones behind them. But don't be too dogmatic about it. For example, if a planting is to be made up entirely of lower-growing annuals (for instance, a border lining a walkway), weaving low-growing campanula through slightly taller salvia or dusty miller would result in a more interesting sight to stroll by or view directly from above.

Spacing and numbers. The assertion that "there is strength in numbers" very definitely applies to flowering annuals. If you want impact, use the spacings recommended in the chapter "Annuals A to Z" (pages 53 to 94), and fill the area to be planted. The result will be a brilliant mass of solid color, with little open soil left for weeds or debris.

A sixpack of Peter Pan zinnias stretched out in a 12-foot-long row looks strangely sparse. Six sixpacks (36 plants) properly spaced in the same area yield a satisfying concentration of vibrant color.

Plant habit and flower texture. Blending and contrasting colors are obviously important to successful flower gardening, but so are mixing and matching plant habits and flower textures. Compare the visual impact of a 10-foot-high sunflower with that of a ground-hugging cascading lobelia. One is an assertively upright sentry, with large, bold leaves and a platterlike circular flower. The other is diminutive, with delicate bloom and an outward-reaching habit. This comparison may be a bit extreme, but it points out how individual plants can contrast in character without reference to color.

Blending annuals with different habits gives each stronger impact. The spires of fairy primrose are more stately when fronted by the bold faces of pansies. The feathery foliage of dusty miller beautifully complements the mounding habit and trumpetlike flowers of petunias. The ever-moving, ribbonlike foliage and spiked seedheads of annual grasses lending graceful movement as well as subtle color to a landscape make a beautiful accent among refined Transvaal daisies. And an even carpet of sweet alyssum can form a perfect foil for the flat flower clusters of sweet William (*Dianthus*).

Proper spacing and a well-planned transition of heights from front to back creates a successful border of ageratum, marigolds (Tagetes), and salvia.

*U*sing Color

Color is what gardening with annuals is all about. Like a painter, a gardener can use annuals in bold or subtle strokes, choosing bright hues or muted tones. The colors are at your fingertips: all you need to do is plant them out.

When pairing different colors, don't shy away from your favorite combinations. A garden should reflect the tastes of the gardener. And don't forget that there is beauty in simplicity. An all-white garden can be a wonderfully cool place to be in midsummer; a planting entirely composed of red zinnias can be a visually stimulating focal point in an otherwise green landscape.

Understanding the Color Wheel

The color wheel picture on the facing page is a rainbow spectrum in a circle. It shows the interrelationships of colors and illustrates color principles that you can reliably apply to planning a flower garden.

Primary. Red, yellow, and blue are called primary colors. All other colors can be produced by various mixtures of these three. Conversely, no mixture of

Generous waves of yellow and orange marigolds (Tagetes) are set off wonderfully by spikes of blue salvia.

other colors will produce pure red, yellow, or blue. These three colors are spaced equally around the color wheel.

Complementary. Colors directly across the wheel—red and green, for example, or blue and orange—are said to be complementary. If you combine annuals of complementary colors, they contrast with each other. Color contrasts—such as blue lobelia in front of a large planting of yellow marigolds—can lead the eye to a certain area: think of a large green tree underplanted with red impatiens.

But proportion is important. Contrasting colors can easily be overused and become visually disruptive. Large plantings of contrasting annuals set side by side—such as orange marigolds next to blue ageratum—can look both boring and slightly disquieting. The same marigolds highlighted with just a flash of ageratum make a much more pleasing sight.

Harmonious. Colors that lie between any two primary colors are said to harmonize with one another. This simply means they are graduated mixtures of those two primary colors. For example, the transition from yellow to red—through yellow-orange, orange, and red-orange—is accomplished by gradually adding more red to yellow. The closer the two colors are in the spectrum, the more harmonious they are.

Gardens planted with harmonious colors can be very attractive, particularly if you want to bring a sense of unity to a landscape without overpowering it.

Warm versus cool. The spectrum divides into two easily recognizable halves: warm colors and cool colors. The warm tones center around orange, the cool ones around blue. The dividing line would be drawn between green and yellow–green on one side and red and red–violet on the other.

The warmth or coolness of colors can affect the emotions of those viewing them. Annuals with warm orange and red flowers could make a hot patio or deck seem even hotter. The same patio planted with blues, violets, and whites can seem cooler and more inviting. A woodsy garden planted in cool blues and violets is extremely subdued and relaxing.

Warm colors also have their place. They have particular impact when viewed from a distance. Red cosmos planted near the rear of a garden immediately attract the eye, while light blue larkspur would not be nearly as noticeable.

Color value: light to dark. Not only does the color wheel show relationships between one color and another, it also shows that a single color has a range of different values from light to dark. Each pure spectrum color in the wheel is identified by name. These colors become lighter in value toward the center of the wheel, as they are diluted with more and more white. Toward the outside of the wheel, as the amount of white decreases, each color becomes darker in value with the addition of black.

No matter how value may vary from light to dark, the color retains the same contrasting and harmonious relationships with others on the wheel. For example, full blue with pale peach is just a variation of the blue-and-orange contrast.

Value affects how a color relates to white. Colors with lighter values harmonize with white, while those with darker values contrast. To illustrate the point, imagine dark red geraniums edged with white violas compared to light pink geraniums edged with the same violas. One look is bold and boisterous, the other soft and subdued.

Never underestimate the power of white flowers.

White reflects more light than any other color. White flowers can brighten the darkest area—even a patio on a moonlit night.

Gray. As the great moderator of color, gray deserves special mention. And when it comes to annuals, gray means dusty miller.

The color gray results from a mixture of any two complementary colors, so it can be employed to tie together otherwise-contrasting colors. Imagine a bed of blue salvia mixed with orange marigolds. Then envision the same colors surrounded by an edging of dusty miller. The contrast still exists, but is subdued by the presence of the gray-leafed plant.

Playing with Color

Now that the color lesson is over, it's time to have fun and let yourself go. You can get ideas for color combinations anywhere: from paintings, public parks, botanical gardens, even other people's gardens. Or try taking your favorite bicolored flower and using its component hues to plan additions and combinations. With all the "instant color" available in nurseries today, you can even check your palette of blooming plants before you buy.

Color Wheel

Color wheel shows primary colors (yellow, red, blue) spaced equidistant around the circle, with the transitional colors that connect them. The pure hue of each color is labeled, the shade of each color is made by the addition of black, and the tint comes when white is added.

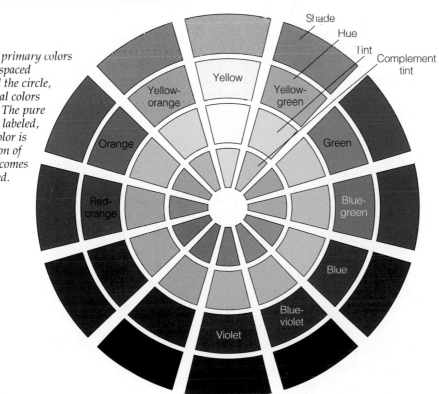

Knowing when an annual blooms and the colors in which it blooms is the key to effectively planning a flower garden. On the following pages are lists of popular annuals according to season of bloom. Also marked are the flower colors each plant has to offer.

Spring performers: nigella and California poppies (Eschscholzia)

Spring

NAME OF PLANT	RED	PINK	YELLOW	ORANGE	BLUE	PURPLE	WHITE	MULTICOLORED	GREEN
Annual grasses									■
Antirrhinum	■	■	■	■		■	■	■	
Arctotis	■	■	■	■		■	■	■	
Brachycome		■			■		■		
Brassica	■	■				■	■	■	■
Calceolaria	■	■	■					■	
Calendula			■	■			■		
Cheiranthus	■	■	■			■			
Chrysanthemum			■				■	■	
Clarkia	■	■	■				■		
Coleus	■	■	■	■			■	■	■
Consolida	■	■			■	■	■		
Cynoglossum		■			■		■		
Dianthus	■	■	■				■	■	
Dimorphotheca	■	■	■	■				■	
Eschscholzia	■	■	■					■	
Felicia					■				
Gazania	■	■	■			■	■	■	
Iberis	■	■				■	■		
Lathyrus	■	■		■	■	■	■	■	
Linum	■	■					■		
Lobularia	■					■	■		
Lychnis		■			■	■	■		
Matthiola	■	■	■			■	■	■	
Myosotis		■			■		■		
Nemesia	■	■	■		■	■	■	■	
Nemophila					■		■		
Nicotiana	■					■	■		■
Nigella		■			■	■	■		
Papaver	■	■	■	■			■		
Pelargonium	■	■		■			■		
Petunia	■	■	■		■	■	■	■	
Primula	■	■	■		■	■	■	■	
Reseda							■		■
Schizanthus	■	■	■			■	■		
Senecio	■	■				■	■	■	
Trachymene					■				
Tropaeolum	■	■	■	■			■		
Viola	■		■	■	■	■	■	■	
Wildflowers	■	■	■	■	■	■	■	■	■

(Continued on page 16)

Wispy blue forget-me-nots (Myosotis) combine with lightly
fragrant sweet alyssum (Lobularia) to celebrate springtime.

Summer

. . . Flower Color by Season

NAME OF PLANT	RED	PINK	YELLOW	ORANGE	BLUE	PURPLE	WHITE	MULTICOLORED	GREEN
Abelmoschus	■	■						■	
Ageratum		■			■	■	■		
Alcea	■	■	■	■		■	■		
Amaranthus	■		■						
Ammi							■		
Ammobium							■		
Anchusa					■				
Annual grasses									■
Antirrhinum	■	■	■	■		■	■	■	
Arctotis	■	■	■	■		■	■	■	
Begonia	■	■					■		
Brachycome		■			■		■		
Browallia					■	■	■		
Bupleurum			■						
Calceolaria	■	■	■					■	
Calendula			■	■			■		
Callistephus	■	■			■	■	■		
Campanula		■			■		■		
Capsicum	■		■	■					
Carthamus			■	■					
Catharanthus	■	■				■	■		
Celosia	■	■	■	■		■			
Centaurea		■			■	■	■		
Chrysanthemum							■	■	
Clarkia	■	■	■			■	■		
Cleome		■	■			■	■		
Coleus	■	■	■	■		■	■	■	■
Convolvulus	■	■			■	■	■		
Coreopsis	■		■	■				■	
Cosmos	■	■	■	■		■	■	■	
Crepis	■	■					■		
Cuphea	■								
Dahlia	■	■	■	■		■	■	■	
Dianthus	■	■	■				■	■	
Diascia		■							
Dyssodia			■						
Eschscholzia	■	■	■	■					
Euphorbia							■	■	■
Felicia					■				
Gaillardia	■		■	■				■	
Gazania	■	■	■	■		■	■	■	
Gerbera	■	■	■	■			■		
Gilia					■				
Gomphrena	■	■		■		■	■		
Gypsophila	■	■					■		
Helianthus			■	■				■	
Helichrysum	■	■	■	■			■		
Heliotropium					■	■	■		
Helipterum	■	■	■				■		
Iberis	■	■				■	■		
Impatiens	■	■		■		■	■	■	

Among summer pastels: blue salvia and pink lychnis

NAME OF PLANT	RED	PINK	YELLOW	ORANGE	BLUE	PURPLE	WHITE	MULTICOLORED	GREEN
Ipomoea	■	■			■	■	■		
Kochia	■								■
Lathyrus	■	■		■	■	■	■	■	
Lavatera	■	■					■		
Limonium	■	■	■	■	■		■		
Linaria	■	■	■	■	■	■	■	■	
Linum	■	■					■		
Lobelia	■	■				■	■		
Lobularia	■	■				■	■		
Lychnis		■			■		■		
Mimulus	■		■	■				■	
Mirabilis	■	■	■				■	■	
Moluccella									■
Nemesia	■	■			■	■	■	■	
Nicotiana	■	■				■	■		■
Nierembergia					■	■	■		
Papavor	■	■		■	■		■	■	
Pelargonium	■	■		■		■	■	■	
Pentzia				■					
Petunia	■	■	■	■	■	■	■	■	

NAME OF PLANT	RED	PINK	YELLOW	ORANGE	BLUE	PURPLE	WHITE	MULTICOLORED	GREEN
Phlox	■	■				■	■	■	
Portulaca	■	■	■	■			■		
Proboscidea		■				■	■		
Rudbeckia	■		■	■				■	
Salpiglossis	■	■	■			■	■	■	
Salvia	■				■	■	■		
Sanvitalia			■	■			■		
Scabiosa	■	■			■	■	■		
Schizanthus	■	■				■	■		
Tagetes	■		■	■			■	■	
Talinum		■							
Thunbergia			■	■			■		
Tithonia				■					
Torenia	■	■				■	■	■	
Trachymene						■			
Tropaeolum	■	■	■	■			■	■	
Verbena	■	■			■	■	■	■	
Viola	■	■	■	■	■	■	■	■	
Wildflowers	■	■	■	■	■	■	■	■	■
Zinnia	■	■	■	■		■	■	■	■

(Continued on next page)

'Old Mexico' zinnia blooms in bright shades of yellow, orange, and red throughout summer.

Fall

NAME OF PLANT	RED	PINK	YELLOW	ORANGE	BLUE	PURPLE	WHITE	MULTICOLORED	GREEN
Abelmoschus	■	■						■	
Ageratum		■			■	■	■		
Amaranthus	■		■						
Annual grasses									■
Begonia	■	■					■		
Brassica	■	■				■	■	■	■
Calendula			■	■			■		
Catharanthus	■	■				■	■		
Chrysanthemum			■				■	■	
Coleus	■	■	■	■		■	■	■	■
Cosmos	■	■	■	■		■	■	■	
Cuphea	■								
Dahlia	■	■	■	■		■	■	■	
Dyssodia			■						
Euphorbia							■	■	■
Gaillardia	■		■	■				■	
Gerbera	■	■	■	■			■		
Gomphrena	■	■			■		■	■	

NAME OF PLANT	RED	PINK	YELLOW	ORANGE	BLUE	PURPLE	WHITE	MULTICOLORED	GREEN
Impatiens	■	■		■		■	■	■	
Ipomoea	■	■				■	■	■	
Kochia	■								■
Lobelia	■	■				■		■	
Lobularia	■	■					■	■	
Mirabilis	■	■	■					■	■
Pelargonium	■	■		■			■	■	
Petunia	■	■	■		■	■	■	■	
Phlox	■	■					■	■	■
Portulaca	■	■	■	■			■		
Salvia	■					■	■		
Sanvitalia			■	■					
Scabiosa	■	■				■	■	■	
Tagetes	■	■		■			■	■	
Torenia	■					■	■	■	
Verbena	■					■	■	■	
Wildflowers	■	■	■	■	■	■	■	■	
Zinnia	■	■	■	■		■	■	■	■

Most summer annuals, like these petunias and marigolds, bloom until the first frost.

Winter

NAME OF PLANT	RED	PINK	YELLOW	ORANGE	BLUE	PURPLE	WHITE	MULTICOLORED	GREEN
Antirrhinum	■	■	■	■		■	■	■	
Brassica	■	■				■	■	■	■
Calendula			■	■			■		
Chrysanthemum			■				■	■	
Dimorphotheca	■	■	■	■			■		
Linaria	■	■	■	■	■	■	■	■	
Lobularia	■	■				■	■		
Lychnis		■			■		■		
Nemesia	■	■	■		■	■	■	■	
Primula	■	■	■	■	■	■	■		
Schizanthus	■	■				■	■		
Senecio	■	■			■	■		■	
Tropaeolum	■	■	■	■			■		
Viola	■		■	■	■	■		■	
Wildflowers	■	■	■	■	■	■	■	■	

When planted in fall, cool-season annuals such as calendula, sweet alyssum (Lobularia), and linaria will bloom during winter in mild winter climates.

Pansies (Viola) offer mild-winter gardens a rainbow of color.

Where & How to Use Annuals

Each annual has its own cultural needs of sun or shade, moist soil or dry. Each also has a unique growth habit that makes it appropriate for certain garden situations. Grouping plants with similar needs and selecting ones that fit well in a particular location or with your style of gardening are important steps in planning a successful flower garden. Here and on the following 15 pages are lists of annuals grouped by cultural needs, growth habits, and specific uses to help you make the right choices.

This sunny summer combination stars red zinnias, white cosmos, and yellow sunflowers (Helianthus) and marigolds (Tagetes).

Annuals for Full Sun

These are annuals that flower best when planted where they can receive at least 6 hours of direct sunlight a day. Many can be grown in areas with light shade for a portion of the day, but they may bloom less, become more leggy and less compact, or be subject to mildew.

Abelmoschus *(Silk flower)*
Ageratum *(Floss flower)*
Alcea *(Hollyhock)*
Amaranthus *(Love-lies-bleeding)*
Ammi *(White lace flower)*
Ammobium *(Winged everlasting)*
Anchusa *(Summer forget-me-not)*
Annual grasses
Antirrhinum *(Snapdragon)*
Arctotis *(African daisy)*
Brachycome *(Swan River daisy)*
Brassica *(Flowering cabbage and kale)*
Bupleurum
Calendula
Callistephus *(China aster)*
Campanula *(Canterbury bells)*
Capsicum *(Ornamental pepper)*
Carthamus *(Safflower)*
Catharanthus *(Madagascar periwinkle)*
Celosia *(Cockscomb)*
Centaurea
Cheiranthus *(Wallflower)*
Chrysanthemum
Clarkia
Cleome *(Spider flower)*
Consolida *(Larkspur)*
Convolvulus *(Dwarf morning glory)*
Coreopsis
Cosmos
Crepis *(Hawk's beard)*
Cuphea *(Firecracker plant)*
Cynoglossum *(Chinese forget-me-not)*
Dahlia
Dianthus
Diascia *(Twinspur)*
Dimorphotheca *(African daisy)*
Dyssodia *(Dahlberg daisy)*
Eschscholzia *(California poppy)*

Flowering in mixed colors, zinnias, purple cockscomb (Celosia), and blue salvia stand up to heat and bright sun.

Euphorbia (Snow-on-the-mountain)
Felicia (Blue marguerite)
Gaillardia (Blanket flower)
Gazania
Gerbera (Transvaal daisy)
Gilia (Blue thimble flower)
Gomphrena (Globe amaranth)
Gypsophila (Baby's breath)
Helianthus (Sunflower)
Helichrysum (Strawflower)
Heliotropium (Heliotrope)
Helipterum (Strawflower)
Iberis (Candytuft)
Ipomoea (Morning glory)
Kochia (Summer cypress)
Lathyrus (Sweet pea)
Lavatera (Tree mallow)
Limonium (Statice)
Linaria (Toadflax)
Linum (Flax)
Lobelia
Lobularia (Sweet alyssum)
Lychnis
Matthiola (Stock)
Mirabilis (Four o'clock)
Moluccella (Bells-of-Ireland)
Nemesia

Nemophila (Baby blue eyes)
Nicotiana (Flowering tobacco)
Nierembergia (Cup flower)
Nigella (Love-in-a-mist)
Papaver (Poppy)
Pelargonium (Geranium)
Pentzia (Gold button)
Petunia
Phlox
Portulaca (Moss rose)
Proboscidea (Unicorn plant)
Reseda (Mignonette)
Rudbeckia (Black-eyed Susan)
Salpiglossis (Painted-tongue)
Salvia
Sanvitalia (Creeping zinnia)
Scabiosa (Pincushion flower)
Tagetes (Marigold)
Talinum (Jewels of Opar)
Thunbergia (Black-eyed Susan vine)
Tithonia (Mexican sunflower)
Torenia (Wishbone flower)
Trachymene (Blue lace flower)
Tropaeolum (Nasturtium)
Verbena
Viola (Pansy and viola)
Zinnia

Annuals for Shady Gardens

The first step toward growing flowers in shade successfully is to recognize the type of shade you have. Types include filtered shade from a high canopy of trees, dense shade on the north side of a house, morning shade followed by afternoon sun, and afternoon shade preceded by morning sun. And what's shady in spring may be sunny in summer. It is fair to say that there are almost as many kinds of shade as there are gardens that are shady. Keeping a record of what plants work well in the shady parts of your own garden is the best way to ensure success from year to year.

Few plants will grow in very dense shade. However, many sun-loving plants can tolerate shade for part of the day. Here are annuals that will bloom in shade. Those marked with an asterisk (*) are most reliable in dense shade.

*Begonia (Bedding begonia)**
Browallia
Calceolaria
Campanula (Canterbury bells)
Cheiranthus (Wallflower)
Cleome (Spider flower)
*Coleus**
Consolida (Larkspur)
Cynoglossum (Chinese forget-me-not)
Gerbera (Transvaal daisy)
*Impatiens**
Linaria (Toadflax)
Lobelia
Lobularia (Sweet alyssum)
*Mimulus (Monkey flower)**
*Myosotis (Forget-me-not)**
Nemophila (Baby blue eyes)
Nicotiana (Flowering tobacco)
Nigella (Love-in-a-mist)
Pelargonium (Geranium)
Primula (Primrose)
Schizanthus (Butterfly flower)
*Senecio (Cineraria)**
Thunbergia (Black-eyed Susan vine)
*Torenia (Wishbone flower)**
Viola (Pansy and viola)

Violas and monkey flowers (Mimulus) bloom reliably in partial shade.

Potted fairy primrose (Primula) is ideal for a shady entryway.

Annuals for Hot, Dry Places

Most annuals require regular irrigation to bloom consistently. However, some perform better where heat and/or sunlight are intense and watering irregular.

Amaranthus (Love-lies-bleeding)
Annual grasses
Arctotis (African daisy)
Brachycome (Swan River daisy)
Centaurea (Cornflower and dusty miller)
Convolvulus (Dwarf morning glory)
Coreopsis
Dimorphotheca (African daisy)
Dyssodia (Dahlberg daisy)
Eschscholzia (California poppy)
Euphorbia (Snow-on-the-mountain)
Gaillardia (Blanket flower)
Gazania
Gomphrena (Globe amaranth)
Gypsophila (Baby's breath)
Iberis (Candytuft)
Kochia (Summer cypress)
Mirabilis (Four o'clock)
Phlox
Portulaca (Moss rose)
Rudbeckia (Black-eyed Susan)
Salvia
Sanvitalia (Creeping zinnia)
Tagetes (Marigold)
Tithonia (Mexican sunflower)
Tropaeolun. (Nasturtium)
Verbena

Verbena is a reliable bloomer for a hot, dry planting site.

African daisy (Arctotis) does best in dry soils.

Love-lies-bleeding (Amaranthus) and marigolds (Tagetes) thrive in heat.

Annuals for Containers

Growing annuals in containers has many advantages. Most important is that containers are mobile. You can keep them in an out-of-the-way spot while the plants are filling out, then move them to center stage at bloom time. Containers also let you enjoy flowers where there is little space or open soil, such as on patios or decks or in entryways. And containers come in a wide range of sizes, colors, and styles that can complement your plants as well as your garden.

As long as you use a good soil mix (see page 49 for information on container soils), you can grow almost any annual in a container. However, shorter varieties and ones with neat, compact habits and long bloom periods are most satisfactory. You can use one plant per pot, or mix and match colors and plant textures.

Try to mix plants with similar sun requirements and bloom periods. Remember that containers dry out quickly and need to be watered more often than flower beds. Container-grown annuals also need more frequent applications of nitrogen fertilizer (for more information on container care, see page 49).

Try to keep taller plants in the middle and shorter or cascading plants (see the list of annuals for hanging baskets on page 26) near the edge of the container. And space plants a little closer than you would in open ground.

Ageratum (Floss flower)
Annual grasses
Antirrhinum (Snapdragon)
Begonia (Bedding begonia)
Brachycome (Swan River daisy)
Brassica (Flowering cabbage and kale)
Browallia
Calceolaria
Calendula
Callistephus (China aster)
Campanula (Canterbury bells)
Capsicum (Ornamental pepper)
Catharanthus (Madagascar periwinkle)
Celosia (Cockscomb)
Centaurea (Dusty miller)
Chrysanthemum
Coleus
Convolvulus (Dwarf morning glory)
Coreopsis
Cosmos
Cuphea (Firecracker plant)
Dahlia
Dianthus
Diascia (Twinspur)
Dyssodia (Dahlberg daisy)
Felicia (Blue marguerite)
Gaillardia (Blanket flower)

The mounding habit of petunias makes them ideal for growing in containers.

Gazania
Gerbera *(Transvaal daisy)*
Gomphrena *(Globe amaranth)*
Helichrysum *(Strawflower)*
Heliotropium *(Heliotrope)*
Iberis *(Candytuft)*
Impatiens
Kochia *(Summer cypress)*
Lathyrus *(Sweet pea)*
Lobelia
Lobularia *(Sweet alyssum)*
Lychnis
Matthiola *(Stock)*
Mimulus *(Monkey flower)*
Nemesia
Nicotiana *(Flowering tobacco)*
Nierembergia *(Cup flower)*
Papaver *(Poppy)*

Pelargonium *(Geranium)*
Petunia
Phlox
Portulaca *(Moss rose)*
Primula *(Primrose)*
Rudbeckia *(Black-eyed Susan)*
Salvia
Sanvitalia *(Creeping zinnia)*
Schizanthus *(Butterfly flower)*
Senecio *(Cineraria)*
Tagetes *(Marigold)*
Thunbergia *(Black-eyed Susan vine)*
Torenia *(Wishbone flower)*
Tropaeolum *(Nasturtium)*
Verbena
Viola *(Pansy and viola)*
Zinnia

Colorful planter bursts with pink petunias, cascading lobelia, and focal-point marigolds (Tagetes).

Containers brimming with annual color make this garden a dazzler. Petunias, marigolds (Tagetes), lobelia, dusty miller (Centaurea), and dwarf dahlias—to name a few—are all on display here.

Compact marigolds (Tagetes), pansies (Viola), salvia, and nemesia fill a hanging wicker basket.

Annuals for Hanging Baskets

Hanging baskets bring flowers to eye level, where they can be enjoyed up close. Plants with spreading, mounding, or very compact habits are best suited to this aerial form of gardening. For more information on gardening in hanging baskets, see page 49.

Begonia *(Bedding begonia)*
Brachycome *(Swan River daisy)*
Browallia
Campanula
Chrysanthemum
Convolvulus *(Dwarf morning glory)*
Dianthus
Dyssodia *(Dahlberg daisy)*
Impatiens
Lobelia
Lobularia *(Sweet alyssum)*
Mimulus *(Monkey flower)*
Nemesia
Nierembergia *(Cup flower)*
Pelargonium *(Ivy geranium)*
Petunia
Phlox
Portulaca *(Moss rose)*
Primula *(Primrose)*
Salvia
Sanvitalia *(Creeping zinnia)*
Schizanthus *(Butterfly flower)*
Tagetes *(Marigold)*
Thunbergia *(Black-eyed Susan vine)*
Tropaeolum *(Nasturtium)*
Verbena
Viola *(Pansy and viola)*

The spreading habit of Swan River daisy (Brachycome) makes it grow softly around a hanging container.

Annuals for Edgings

These are neat, low-growing annuals or types that are available in low-growing varieties. For the most part, they stay under 12 inches high and are ideal for growing in front of taller plants, in narrow spaces or along walkways, or near the edges of containers.

Ageratum *(Floss flower)*
Annual grasses
Antirrhinum *(Snapdragon)*
Begonia *(Bedding begonia)*
Brachycome *(Swan River daisy)*
Brassica *(Flowering cabbage and kale)*
Browallia
Calendula
Callistephus *(China aster)*
Catharanthus *(Madagascar periwinkle)*
Centaurea *(Dusty miller)*
Chrysanthemum
Coleus
Convolvulus *(Dwarf morning glory)*
Crepis *(Hawk's beard)*
Dahlia
Dianthus
Diascia *(Twinspur)*
Dimorphotheca *(African daisy)*
Dyssodia *(Dahlberg daisy)*
Felicia *(Blue marguerite)*
Gazania
Gerbera *(Transvaal daisy)*
Gomphrena *(Globe amaranth)*
Helichrysum *(Strawflower)*
Iberis *(Candytuft)*
Linaria *(Toadflax)*
Lobelia
Lobularia *(Sweet alyssum)*
Lychnis
Mimulus *(Monkey flower)*
Nemesia
Nierembergia *(Cup flower)*
Petunia
Phlox
Portulaca *(Moss rose)*
Primula *(Primrose)*
Salvia
Sanvitalia *(Creeping zinnia)*
Schizanthus *(Butterfly flower)*
Tagetes *(Marigold)*
Torenia *(Wishbone flower)*
Tropaeolum *(Nasturtium)*
Verbena
Viola *(Pansy and viola)*
Zinnia

Ground-hugging purple and white sweet alyssum (Lobularia) is a perfect edging. It is grown here with Oriental poppies.

Compact blue ageratum edges silvery dusty miller (Centaurea) with accents of red salvia.

Annuals for Cut Flowers

Whether you grow flowers for cutting in a border mixed with other flowers or design a bed just to supply bouquets, these are the annuals to choose for cut arrangements. For longest-lasting bouquets, cut the flowers in the evening, remove lower leaves, and place stems immediately in water. Some varieties do best with stem ends seared; check the encyclopedia entries. Change the water in the vase frequently.

Sunflowers (Helianthus), shown here in a generous-looking bouquet of mixed varieties, make a bold statement as cut flowers.

'Selma-Sonnen'

'California Black'

'Abendsonne'

'Autumn Beauty'

'Sungold'

'Sunlight'

'Stella'

'Luna'

'Primrose'

Ageratum (Floss flower, tall types)
Ammi (White lace flower)
Annual grasses
Antirrhinum (Snapdragon)
Browallia
Bupleurum
Calendula
Callistephus (China aster)
Campanula (Canterbury bells)
Carthamus (Safflower)
Celosia (Cockscomb)
Centaurea (Cornflower and sweet sultan)
Chrysanthemum
Clarkia
Cleome (Spider flower)
Consolida (Larkspur)
Coreopsis
Cosmos
Cynoglossum (Chinese forget-me-not)
Dahlia
Dianthus
Eschscholzia (California poppy)
Euphorbia (Snow-on-the-mountain)
Gaillardia (Blanket flower)
Gerbera (Transvaal daisy)
Gomphrena (Globe amaranth)
Gypsophila (Baby's breath)
Helianthus (Sunflower)
Helichrysum (Strawflower)
Heliotropium (Heliotrope)
Kochia (Burning bush)
Lathyrus (Sweet pea)
Limonium (Statice)
Lychnis
Matthiola (Stock)
Moluccella (Bells-of-Ireland)
Myosotis (Forget-me-not)
Papaver (Poppy)
Pentzia (Gold button)
Phlox
Rudbeckia (Black-eyed Susan)
Salpiglossis
Scabiosa (Pincushion flower)
Tagetes (Marigold)
Talinum (Jewels of Opar)
Tithonia (Mexican sunflower)
Trachymene (Blue lace flower)
Viola (Pansy and viola)
Zinnia

China asters (Callistephus) make long-lasting cut flowers.

Zinnias can be mainstays in a cutting garden.

New Guinea impatiens offer interesting leaf texture as well as flower color. Some are variegated.

Annuals with Colorful Foliage

Plants with colorful leaves can be stunning by themselves. Or use them to highlight or contrast with other flowering plants in beds or bouquets.

Amaranthus *(Love-lies-bleeding)*
Ammobium *(Winged everlasting)*
Begonia *(Bedding begonia)*
Brassica *(Flowering cabbage and kale)*
Centaurea *(Dusty miller)*
Coleus
Euphorbia *(Snow-on-the-mountain)*
Impatiens *(New Guinea impatiens)*
Pelargonium *(Zonal geranium)*

Painted in shades of green to maroon, coleus leaves mix well with impatiens. It's best to pinch off coleus flowers.

Tall Annuals

These are annuals to use at the back of a border for vertical emphasis, or as background plants. Most grow, or are available in varieties that grow, over 3 feet tall.

Alcea (Hollyhock)
Amaranthus (Love-lies-bleeding)
Annual grasses
Antirrhinum (Snapdragon)
Campanula (Canterbury bells)
Celosia (Cockscomb)
Clarkia
Cleome (Spider flower)
Cosmos
Consolida (Larkspur)
Helianthus (Sunflower)
Lavatera (Tree mallow)
Moluccella (Bells-of-Ireland)
Nicotiana (Flowering tobacco)
Tagetes (Marigold)
Tithonia (Mexican sunflower)
Zinnia

Old-fashioned hollyhocks (Alcea) make a stunning vertical statement, ideal for softening a large wall.

Tall snapdragons (Antirrhinum) provide a perfect background for lower and slightly lighter-toned pansies (Viola).

Annuals for Dried Bouquets

Often called everlastings, the flowers or seed heads of these plants will retain their color when dried if you hang them upside down in a cool, dark, well-ventilated place. Many other annual flowers can be dried using silica gels or by pressing.

Ammobium *(Winged everlasting)*
Annual grasses
Carthamus *(Safflower)*
Celosia *(Cockscomb)*
Centaurea *(Cornflower)*
Crepis *(Hawk's beard)*
Gomphrena *(Globe amaranth)*
Gypsophila *(Annual baby's breath)*
Helianthus *(Sunflower)*
Helichrysum *(Strawflower)*
Helipterum *(Strawflower)*
Limonium *(Statice)*
Moluccella *(Bells-of-Ireland)*
Nigella *(Love-in-a-mist)*
Pentzia *(Gold button)*
Proboscidea *(Unicorn plant)*
Scabiosa *(Pincushion flower)*

Strawflower (Helipterum) retains color intensity when dried.

The dainty flowers of gomphrena and the bold blossoms of cockscomb (Celosia) are old standbys for everlasting bouquets.

Annuals with Fragrant Flowers

When you plant fragrant flowers, you're inviting another one of your senses into the garden, increasing
the pleasures it can offer you. These annuals have
fragrant flowers—some faintly aromatic, others
sweetly alluring. Plants with stronger fragrance are
marked with an asterisk (*). Place them along walkways, around decks or patios, near windows, or in
any other spot where they can be enjoyed often.

Centaurea (Sweet sultan)
Cheiranthus (Wallflower)
*Dianthus**
Heliotropium (Heliotrope)*
Lathyrus (Sweet pea)*
Matthiola (Stock)*
Mirabilis (Four o'clock)
Nicotiana (Flowering tobacco)
Petunia
Primula (Primrose)
Reseda (Mignonette)*
Tropaeolum (Nasturtium)

*Few flowers can match the wonderfully rich, sweet fragrance
of a crowd of sweet peas (Lathyrus).*

Stock (Matthiola), fronted by yellow pansies (Viola) here, has strong, spicy fragrance.

Wildflowers & Annuals That Naturalize

In the true sense of the word, a wildflower is a plant that is native to your area—and therefore supremely well adapted to it. But with wildflower mixes on the shelves of almost every garden center today, all a plant really needs to be called a wildflower is to be easy to grow from seed and capable of naturalizing either by reseeding or being perennial.

Wildflower gardens can be effective, especially in a large area that is difficult to maintain. Seed is usually sown over a prepared planting bed in late fall or early spring. Wildflowers can also be interspersed with cultivated plants in beds and borders. But take care to plant species that are suited to your specific area.

There are a number of good resources to help you find which plants are best grown as wildflowers in your area. The National Wildflower Research Cen-

ter (2600 FM 973 North, Austin, TX 78725) has a clearinghouse for information on current research and wildflower projects in each state and can supply advice on seed sources, recommended species, and appropriate planting procedures. The Soil Conservation Society of America (7515 Northeast Ankeny Rd., Ankeny, IA 50021-9764) and the Nature Conservancy (1815 North Lynn St., Arlington, VA 22209) also offer information on wildflowers and native plants. Many states have native plant societies that can provide information on regional wildflowers.

On the facing page are annuals that will reliably reseed themselves. In areas where the ground does not freeze, most can be counted on to bloom year after year. They are best used in open areas where neatness or a formal look is not important. Many need regular watering.

Red and pink Shirley poppies (Papaver), orange California poppies (Eschscholzia), and baby blue eyes (Nemophila) form a delicately beautiful spring wildflower meadow.

California poppies (Eschscholzia) and calendulas are two annuals that reseed and bloom year after year.

Brachycome (Swan River daisy)
Calendula
Centaurea (Cornflower)
Cheiranthus (Wallflower)
Chrysanthemum
Clarkia
Consolida (Larkspur)
Cosmos
Dimorphotheca (African daisy)
Eschscholzia (California poppy)
Gilia (Blue thimble flower)

Helianthus (Sunflower)
Lavatera (Tree mallow)
Linaria (Toadflax)
Linum (Flax)
Lobularia (Sweet alyssum)
Mirabilis (Four o'clock)
Myosotis (Forget-me-not)
Nemophila (Baby blue eyes)
Papaver (Shirley poppy)
Phlox
Tropaeolum (Nasturtium)

How to Grow Annuals

CARE FROM SEED TO BLOOM

*F*lowering annuals are the plant world's instant gratifiers. Whether you start them from seed or buy them in bloom, they perform very quickly, with only one season to run their course. Like sprinters, they race from germination to flowering, then set new seed to begin the cycle again. Give these botanic athletes the right exposure, good nutrients, and con- sistent conditioning, and they'll reward you with a brilliant floral display at the finish.

Impatiens

Nurseries and garden centers provide ideas, seeds, and plants to start you on the road to a colorful garden.

Planting Cycle

Compared with almost all other plants, the life cycle of an annual is very short. Although the name suggests that such plants live a year, in the garden many won't survive even half that long. Once their blooming cycle is over, most will be pulled, whether still living or not, to make room for the next season's flowers.

Because of this abbreviated cycle, gardening with annuals is more exacting than with plants that live for years. If you make a miscalculation growing a flowering shrub, you probably have plenty of time to correct it. But make a mistake with an annual, and you may have struck out.

Annuals can be purchased from the nursery in a variety of containers. From front to back: six-packs, 4-inch pots, pressed fiber pots, cell-packs, hanging baskets, and gallon pots.

That doesn't mean annuals are hard to grow; in fact, they are relatively easy. What it does mean is that your success—and, generally, the amount of bloom produced—depends heavily on the care you take in raising or purchasing healthy seedlings; choosing an appropriate planting site; preparing the soil; and providing adequate moisture, nutrients, and pest control. For the best bloom, most annuals need to grow vigorously throughout their cycle. Let them stall from a lack of any of their necessities, and you probably won't have time to set things right.

Where to Plant

Most gardeners know where they want to plant annuals, so the real question becomes which annuals will grow best in that location. Note how much sun your planting area receives and match that exposure and your cultural practices with the needs of plants described in the next section of this book.

There are some planting locations to avoid. Few of the annuals described in this book can thrive in dense shade or in soils heavily infiltrated with roots of trees or shrubs. Sometimes you can prune a tree to let more light reach the ground beneath it. But if the soil is full of greedy roots, consider growing annuals in containers.

Remember, also, to plant your annuals where you'll see them often and be able to enjoy your garden's success.

When to Plant

When to sow seeds or set out annuals depends on your climate, growing season, and plant choice.

Cold-winter climates. In much of the country where winters are snowy or at least freezing, annuals bloom from mid-spring through early autumn. Cool-season or hardy annuals (such as pansies, Iceland poppies, flowering cabbage and kale, and primroses) can be planted in very early spring, almost as soon as the ground can be worked. If you delay planting until the weather has settled into mid-spring warmth, you risk disappointment. These plants need to develop roots and foliage during cool weather in order to bloom vigorously as the days grow warmer.

Most summer-flowering or warm-season annuals (such as marigolds, zinnias, and impatiens) should be planted after any danger of frost has passed. Others (such as amaranthus and celosia) grow best when planted later, after the soil has thoroughly warmed.

Mild-winter climates. Where winters are mild—either frost-free or lightly frosty—late winter and early spring are the best times to plant most cool-season annuals, and mid-spring is the time to plant summer or warm-season annuals.

But there is another season in these mild-winter areas: winter. Plants such as cinerarias, Iceland poppies, pansies, and calendulas, to name a few (see page 19 for others), will bloom in winter and early spring if planted in fall. Timing is important. Plant while the days are still warm enough to encourage growth, but while day length is decreasing. If you plant too soon, annuals will rush into bloom before they have become established. Plant too late, and you probably won't get any bloom until spring.

Zinnias weave through salvia and petunias.

Average Hard-Frost Dates/* Based on U.S.D.A. weather records

State	Last in Spring	First in Fall	State	Last in Spring	First in Fall	State	Last in Spring	First in Fall
Alabama, N.W.	Mar. 25	Oct. 30	Kansas	Apr. 20	Oct. 15	Ohio, No.	May 6	Oct. 15
Alabama, S.E.	Mar. 8	Nov. 15	Kentucky	Apr. 15	Oct. 20	Ohio, So.	Apr. 20	Oct. 20
Arizona, No.	Apr. 23	Oct. 19				Oklahoma	Apr. 2	Nov. 2
Arizona, So.	Mar. 1	Dec. 1	Louisiana, No.	Mar. 13	Nov. 10	Oregon, W.	Apr. 17	Oct. 25
Arkansas, No.	Apr. 7	Oct. 23	Louisiana, So.	Feb. 20	Nov. 20	Oregon, E.	June 4	Sept. 22
Arkansas, So.	Mar. 25	Nov. 3						
			Maine	May 25	Sept. 25	Pennsylvania, W.	Apr. 20	Oct. 10
California			Maryland	Apr. 19	Oct. 20	Pennsylvania, Cen.	May 1	Oct. 15
Imperial Valley	Jan. 25	Dec. 15	Massachusetts	Apr. 25	Oct. 25	Pennsylvania, E.	Apr. 17	Oct. 15
Interior Valleys	Mar. 1	Nov. 15	Michigan, Upper pen.	May 25	Sept. 15			
Southern Coast	Jan. 15	Dec. 15	Michigan, No.	May 17	Sept. 25	Rhode Island	Apr. 25	Oct. 25
Central Coast	Feb. 25	Dec. 1	Michigan, So.	May 10	Oct. 8			
Mountain Sections	Apr. 25	Sept. 1	Minnesota, No.	May 26	Sept. 15	S. Carolina, N.W.	Apr. 1	Nov. 8
Colorado, West	May 25	Sept. 18	Minnesota, So.	May 11	Oct. 1	S. Carolina, S.E.	Mar. 15	Nov. 15
Colorado, N.E.	May 11	Sept. 27	Mississippi, No.	Mar. 25	Oct. 30	S. Dakota	May 15	Sept. 25
Colorado, S.E.	May 1	Oct. 15	Mississippi, So.	Mar. 15	Nov. 15			
Connecticut	Apr. 25	Oct. 20	Missouri	Apr. 20	Oct. 20	Tennessee	Apr. 10	Oct. 25
			Montana	May 21	Sept. 22	Texas, N.W.	Mar. 21	Nov. 10
Delaware	Apr. 15	Oct. 25				Texas, N.E.	Apr. 15	Nov. 1
District of Columbia	Apr. 11	Oct. 23	Nebraska, W.	May 11	Oct. 4	Texas, So.	Feb. 10	Dec. 15
			Nebraska, E.	Apr. 15	Oct. 15	Utah	Apr. 26	Oct. 19
Florida, No.	Feb. 25	Dec. 5	Nevada, W.	May 19	Sept. 22			
Florida, Cen.	Feb. 11	Dec. 28	Nevada, E.	June 1	Sept. 14	Vermont	May 23	Sept. 25
Florida, South of Lake Okeechobee, almost frost-free			New Hampshire	May 23	Sept. 25	Virginia, No.	Apr. 15	Oct. 25
			New Jersey	Apr. 20	Oct. 25	Virginia, So.	Apr. 10	Oct. 30
Georgia, No.	Apr. 1	Nov. 1	New Mexico, No.	Apr. 23	Oct. 17			
Georgia, So.	Mar. 15	Nov. 15	New Mexico, So.	Apr. 1	Nov. 1	Washington, W.	Apr. 10	Nov. 15
Idaho	May 21	Sept. 22	New York, W.	May 10	Oct. 8	Washington, E.	May 15	Oct. 1
Illinois, No.	May 1	Oct. 8	New York, E.	May 1	Oct. 15	West Virginia, W.	May 1	Oct. 15
Illinois, So.	Apr. 15	Oct. 20	New York, No.	May 15	Oct. 1	West Virginia, E.	May 15	Oct. 1
Indiana, No.	May 1	Oct. 8	N. Carolina, W.	Apr. 15	Oct. 25	Wisconsin, No.	May 17	Sept. 25
Indiana, So.	Apr. 15	Oct. 20	N. Carolina, E.	Apr. 8	Nov. 1	Wisconsin, So.	May 1	Oct. 10
Iowa, No.	May 1	Oct. 2	N. Dakota, W.	May 21	Sept. 13	Wyoming, W.	June 20	Aug. 20
Iowa, So.	Apr. 15	Oct. 9	N. Dakota, E.	May 16	Sept. 20	Wyoming, E.	May 21	Sept. 20

* Allow 10 days either side of above dates to meet local conditions and seasonal differences.

$\mathcal{I}$mproving the Soil

Good garden soil is porous and drains well, but retains sufficient moisture for roots; and it provides ample nutrients to meet the needs of the plants. Preparing such a soil is one of the most important aspects of growing annuals successfully.

Acid or Alkaline? Test Your Soil

Having your soil tested is a sound gardening practice. It can tell you a great deal about your garden's potential. However, it is usually not necessary to test the places where you want to plant annuals unless you suspect a problem. Your local nursery or agricultural extension office can give you general information and advise you on the possible usefulness of a soil test.

Typically, a test reveals the acidity or alkalinity of your soil. This is expressed in pH numbers: pH 7 is neutral, pH greater than 7 is alkaline, and pH less than 7 is acid. Most annuals grow best in neutral or slightly acid soil. As a rule of thumb, high-rainfall areas tend to have acid soils and low-rainfall areas alkaline soils.

Soil tests also point out any deficiencies of major nutrients.

In many states the local agricultural extension office does testing; if not, it can recommend a private laboratory. You can also buy kits through mail-order garden-supply companies and many nurseries that let you test your own soil.

If the test indicates your soil is too acidic, add lime when you prepare for planting. If your soil is too alkaline, add sulfur. Again, your local nursery or agricultural extension office can recommend how much to add. If your soil is deficient in one or more nutrients, add the appropriate fertilizer (see pages 46 to 47) when you prepare the soil.

Well-prepared soil helps ensure a colorful display like this bed of pansies (Viola), stock (Matthiola), sweet alyssum (Lobularia), petunias, and dianthus.

Soil Sense

Garden soils are generally classified as sandy, loamy, or clayey. Sandy soils usually dry out and drain quickly and are often low in nutrients but well aerated. At the opposite extreme, clayey soils take longer to dry and are usually poorly aerated and slow-draining.

In between clayey and sandy soils are loamy soils, made up of a combination of clay and sand particles and organic matter. These are the best to garden in because they hold moisture and nutrients while being well aerated and fast-draining.

Most garden soils fall either toward the sandy or clayey side, but they can easily be improved with the addition of organic soil amendments.

Soil amendments. Many types can help. Peat moss and manures are sold almost everywhere. Compost is available to any gardener willing to take the time to prepare it and can also be purchased packaged in nurseries or in bulk at some waste disposal sites.

Many by-products of regional agriculture and industry are good soil amendments: redwood and fir bark from lumber-producing regions; sawdust; spent mushroom compost; ground corn cobs; apple or grape pomace (the residue from making cider or wine).

If you plan to amend your soil with manure or wood products (bark or sawdust), you'll need to take a few precautions. Fresh manures can actually harm roots: if you use unaged manure, add it to the soil several months before planting. (If you dig in well-aged manure, you can plant right away.)

Wood products need nitrogen to aid their decomposition and will take from the soil whatever nitrogen they need. The result can be nitrogen-deprived plants. Packaged wood products and some that are sold in bulk are usually nitrogen-fortified, so they can be applied directly. But if you use raw or untreated products, add 1 pound of ammonium sulfate for every 1-inch-deep layer of organic material spread over 100 square feet. Scatter the ammonium sulfate over the spread-out organic matter, then dig the mixture into the soil. Wait about a month before planting.

Preparing the Soil

Thorough preparation means adding a 3-inch layer of amendment and repeatedly turning and digging the soil to a depth of at least 12 inches. It's also a good idea to incorporate a complete fertilizer (see page 47) that has a high ratio of phosphorus and potassium—a 5-10-10 formula, for example.

Working ample amounts of organic matter into the soil before planting improves aeration of a clayey soil and moisture-holding capacity of a sandy soil.

Soil is in good condition for digging when it is moist but crumbles easily. Never work a soil that is sticky and saturated with water. You will only compact it—just the opposite of what you're trying to achieve.

For a small area, dig by hand with a spade or spading fork. For a large, open area, use a rotary tiller. If you don't own a rotary tiller, you can rent one at a local rental yard (check in the Yellow Pages of your phone book).

If possible, prepare your soil several weeks before you intend to plant. This will give the amendments time to mellow and settle slightly. You can pull or hoe out any weeds that spring up during this period without having to work around newly set plants. Just before planting, do a final raking to smooth out any humps or hollows.

Seed vs. Transplants

Annuals can be started from either seeds or transplants. Starting from seed takes more time and energy, but it costs less and gives you a much greater variety of plants to choose from. There is also real pleasure to be derived from growing plants all the way from seed to flower.

Starting from seed. Seeds of annuals can either be started indoors in flats or pots (see photo below) or sown directly in the soil where they are to flower. Some annuals are easier to grow from seed than others. Large seeds, like those of nasturtiums, marigolds, and zinnias, germinate quickly and can be started indoors or sown outdoors with little chance of failure. Seed of such annuals as petunias, impatiens, and geraniums are smaller and slower to germinate, and seedlings take longer to reach transplant size. These plants are hardly ever direct-sown. They can be started indoors, but they demand precise growing conditions and vigilant care. Most people prefer to purchase transplants of annuals like these.

Purchasing transplants. Nursery transplants save you time. And with many plants available in bloom, it's possible to visit a nursery in the morning and have a colorful garden in the afternoon. But instant gratification will cost you considerably more than growing plants from seed.

There is one pitfall to avoid when starting with transplants. Make sure you purchase plants that are healthy and growing vigorously. Plants that have yellowing foliage or are leggy, rootbound, or obviously too big for their pots will be slow to get established in the garden. Most will bloom poorly and require constant watering. When you're shopping for transplants, don't be afraid to slip one or two of each kind gently from their containers to examine the roots. If you see a mass of dense, white, tangled roots

Annual seeds can be started indoors in nursery flats or in purchased ready-to-plant peat pots and pressed peat cubes.

Remove plant by gently pressing on bottom of sixpack. Plant in a diamond pattern, using a precut stick for even spacing.

near the outside of the pot, the plant is rootbound. Look for plants with a fine network of roots, and ones with rootballs in which you can still see soil.

Planting Procedures

Be careful to set plants at the proper depth so their roots can spread into the soil. Planting too deep will cause many annuals to rot at their crown. Annuals planted too shallow will dry out quickly. You also want to be sure the soil is settled and firm around the roots.

Dig each planting hole larger than the plant's rootball. Tip the pot on its side and gently remove the plant from the container (with plastic sixpacks, use your thumb to push up from the bottom). Set the plant in the hole, making sure the top of the rootball is even with the surrounding soil surface. Firm soil around the roots and water well.

Starting from Seed

Some annuals, like sweet alyssum, marigolds, and zinnias, are easy to grow from seeds sown directly in ordinary garden soil. When the time is right, you simply scatter the seeds, lightly cover them with soil, and keep them moist; they germinate in just a few days. Seeds of other annuals have more precise requirements regarding soil temperature and light, and are best started indoors. This is a good way to get a jump on the season.

All the information you need for starting seeds can usually be found on the seed packet. You can also check details given in the encyclopedia section of this book, starting on page 53.

The steps for starting seeds are shown in the illustrations below. Use a sterile growing medium such as packaged vermiculite or potting soil. Make sure all pots and containers are clean (if necessary, scrub with a dilute solution of bleach). Choose a warm, well-lit spot; a greenhouse is ideal, but a sunny window can also work well. Be sure to sow at the appropriate depth. After sowing, keep the soil evenly moist. Letting the growing medium dry out will kill the seeds, but overwatering is likely to cause them to rot.

Once the seeds have germinated, the seedlings must receive strong light, or they will become leggy. Many nurseries sell supplemental lighting systems. You can also maintain consistent soil temperatures by installing heating cables, also available in most nurseries.

A week or two before the seedlings are ready to be transplanted outdoors, harden them off by taking them outside each day for periods of gradually increasing length. Start in a shady spot for just a few hours; bit by bit, expose them to more sun until they are used to outdoor conditions.

Sow seeds in flats of sterile soil or in the ground. Keep planting medium moist.

If sowing directly in garden soil, thin seedlings to proper spacing.

If sowing in flats, transplant seedlings to larger pots or into the garden when they develop the first set of true leaves.

Water & Mulch

To grow vigorously and bloom profusely, annuals need adequate soil moisture throughout their life cycle—enough water so plants never wilt, but not so much that the soil remains soggy and the plants drown.

How often to water. Frequency depends on a number of factors. Plants need to be watered more often when they are younger and have not yet fully developed their root systems. They also need more frequent irrigation in hot, sunny, or windy weather than in cool, cloudy, or calm weather. Soil texture can also influence how often you need to water, though with properly amended soil, this becomes less important.

Newly planted annuals require special attention. Recently sown seeds may need to be watered more than twice a day in warm weather. Young seedlings or transplants may need water at least once a day. As plants become established, you can gradually water less frequently.

The best advice in setting up a watering schedule is to be a good observer of both the weather and your plants. Watch for any signs of wilting, especially in hot weather. Get down on your hands and knees and stick your fingers into the soil: when the top 2 or 3 inches is dry, it's time to water.

How much to water. Apply enough to wet the entire root zone. For most annuals, this means to at least 12 to 18 inches. Watering deeply encourages deep rooting, and the deeper the roots go, the less vulnerable they will be to moisture fluctuations at the soil's surface. If you water plants daily but only lightly, they'll establish shallow root systems and be vulnerable to sudden drying out. Instead, water deeply, allow the soil to dry partially, then water deeply again.

To check how deeply water is penetrating, probe the soil with a long screwdriver or narrow rod. It will move more easily through moist soil and become harder to push in dry soil.

Watering Techniques

What's the best way to apply the water? You have a number of choices.

Overhead watering. This can be done by sprinklers or with a hand-held hose. Sprinklers provide more efficient coverage, especially for large plantings.

Overhead watering does have disadvantages. Some flowers (such as zinnias and petunias) are more susceptible to disease if their leaves and flowers are constantly wet. (If you overhead-water, do it early in the day so the foliage can dry by nighttime.) Overhead watering can wash the color from some flowers. And it can cause taller plants to tip over.

Furrows. If you're planting long, narrow rows of annuals, you may want to water them by digging or hoeing 6- to 8-inch-deep furrows or trenches along one or both sides of the row. Then let a hose run in one end of the furrow until it is full.

The problem with furrows is that they need constant maintenance—and long ones must have a gentle slope from one end to the other. In a wide bed or border, the furrow can be difficult to maintain once the plants are large.

Drip irrigation. This is the most efficient way to water. Drip emitters (or perforated tubing) deliver water right where you want it without wasteful run-off or damage to plant foliage. A drip system can easily be hooked up to an automatic timer to keep plants on schedule while you are away. Your local nurseryman or irrigation supply store can help you design an appropriate drip layout.

Mulches

Simply stated, a mulch is a layer of organic material on the surface of the soil. Nature provides this in the form of fallen leaves and twigs. Good gardeners observe the value of this cover and take pains to follow nature's lead.

Why mulch? A layer of organic material spread 2 to 3 inches deep between plants (close to the plant's base without covering it) greatly reduces evaporation from the soil beneath. Thus the soil surface remains moist longer and is not subject to cracking when dried by the sun.

A mulch also keeps soil cooler than if it were left

bare. But if applied too early in the season, when soil is cold, it can delay warming of the soil and slow development of plants. Particularly in cold-winter climates, where you need to make the most of the growing season, you shouldn't apply mulch until spring weather has warmed the soil.

Mulches also help in weed control. Most weed seeds cannot germinate beneath a thick layer of organic material, and any that do sprout and grow are easy to pull because of the mulch's loose texture.

In addition, mulches can have aesthetic value. A uniform layer of organic material looks neat and tidy; it also prevents mud from splashing on foliage and low-growing flowers.

Last but certainly not least, a mulch improves the quality of the soil beneath it. Organic matter gradually decomposes and becomes incorporated into the upper inches of the soil, improving its texture and ability to assimilate water. When it's time to change plants in a bed, you can work the soil to further incorporate the mulch and improve soil texture.

Mulching materials. Mulch must be loose or coarse enough for water to penetrate. This rules out anything that compacts into an airless mass when moistened—thin-textured leaves or a thick layer of grass clippings, for example. Beyond this restriction, though, your choices are quite varied. Wood by-products (see soil amendments on page 41) and bark chips are widely used, as is compost. Pine needles are popular where they're available. You can even use grass clippings if you spread them among the plants one thin layer at a time, allowing each layer to dry before adding another.

Some agricultural by-products also make excellent mulches—grape pomace and rice hulls, for example.

When woven through annuals, ooze tubes apply water to roots at a slow, even pace. Water goes only where it's needed; none is wasted. And, since foliage stays dry, chance for disease is reduced.

$\mathscr{N}$utrients & Fertilizers

To grow vigorously and stay healthy, plants need adequate nutrients, most of which they extract from the soil. But if the soil can't provide enough nutrients, the gardener must step in and apply supplementary fertilizer (popularly termed "plant food").

Newly planted annuals, especially, need a steady and balanced diet to reach a floriferous maturity. Three nutrients—nitrogen, phosphorus, and potassium—are needed in quantity. There are about six minor nutrients that also are important but needed in far smaller amounts. In addition, various trace elements are required—but in minute quantities. The role that each of the three major nutrients plays is described in "A Fertilizer Primer" on the facing page.

Fertilizer Choices

Most gardeners prefer the convenience of a complete fertilizer—one that includes each of the three major nutrients. You can also provide each of the "major three" separately: blood meal to supply nitrogen, bone meal for phosphorus, and ground rock potash for potassium. But before you proceed to the fertilizer section of your nursery, there's more to know about available types.

Dry and liquid. The boxes and bags of fertilizers on nursery shelves contain dry fertilizers. Many are complete fertilizers in granular and pellet form; they dissolve over a period of time after being mixed into the soil or applied to the surface. Some dry fertilizers are single-nutrient types that are also meant to be mixed into the soil or applied to its surface.

Liquid fertilizer and soluble granules are intended to be dissolved in water (according to label directions) and added to the soil. These may also be complete fertilizers or single-nutrient types (in this case, usually nitrogen sources, such as fish emulsion).

When preparing the soil for planting annuals, dry fertilizers are an obvious choice. Many gardeners prefer to continue with dry fertilizers as they are needed during the growing season (see "Timing the Applications" on the facing page) because they are relatively quick to apply, generally less expensive than liquids, and simple to use. If, however, you apply them unevenly or too heavily, you can burn plant foliage.

Liquid fertilizers are deservedly popular for container-grown annuals. If water can reach all the roots confined in a container in a matter of minutes, a liquid fertilizer can act as a quick tonic. Even though nitrogen not taken up by the roots will be leached out by subsequent waterings, it is little extra trouble to mix and use a liquid fertilizer repeatedly during the growing season as you water your containers.

Liquid fertilizers can be just as effective for plants in the ground. Nurseries now carry many ready-to-use products that come in hose-end sprayers. No mixing is necessary; all you do is attach them to your hose, turn on the water, and spray the fertilizer on the plants. Even though you pay a high price for the amount of nitrogen in ready-to-use fertilizers, you gain much in convenience. Liquid fertilizers that contain urea can also supply nitrogen to the plant through its leaves. Called foliar feeding, such supplementation can be a good way to give annuals a quick boost.

Some liquid fertilizers (not fish emulsion) can be applied through drip-irrigation systems or hose-end sprinklers via fertilizer injectors. These allow you to feed while you water. Your local nursery or irrigation supply store can suggest which type of equipment would best suit your system.

Slow-release. Gaining in popularity and availability are various dry fertilizers that are categorically termed slow-, controlled-, or timed-release. In one way or another, these resist or control the leaching out of nutrients by water. One application will slowly but steadily release nutrients with each watering over a specific period of time. The chief benefit of these fertilizers, though, is sustained release of nitrogen— the most-needed major nutrient, and the one that is most easily leached from the soil. And while they cost more than other kinds of fertilizer, you can weigh this against the small amount you use in a given season and the time you save.

The forerunner to these fertilizers was the urea-formaldehyde type (called urea or urea-form), which gave a sustained nitrogen release because it broke down slowly in the soil. Any fertilizer that contains nitrogen in the form of urea (this is stated on the package) yields a more sustained nitrogen release than fertilizers that contain nitrogen in nitrate or ammoniac form.

Directions on the packages of slow-release fertilizers clearly state the amount to use and when to reapply. These fertilizers are equally useful for growing annuals in the ground and in containers. However, many slow-release fertilizers don't begin to release nutrients for a week or two after application. Others release nutrients more slowly in cool weather. To avoid lag times, many gardeners use them in conjunction with light applications of faster-acting fertilizers.

Timing the Applications

For colorful results, most annuals need a steady supply of nutrients from planting time through the bloom period (a few annuals, such as California poppies, asters, and schizanthus, prefer infertile soil). If you add a complete fertilizer when you prepare the soil, there should be enough nutrients to keep the plants growing vigorously for about the first 6 weeks, at which point you should apply a further nutrient boost—dry, liquid, or controlled-release. How often you feed plants thereafter depends on which kind of fertilizer you plan to use.

Liquids should be repeated every 2 weeks (or every 7 to 10 days at half strength). How often you apply a dry fertilizer depends on its strength; the package directions will suggest timing and quantity. As for controlled-release fertilizers, a single application in conjunction with a liquid feeding may be enough in areas where growing seasons are short; use no more than two applications where growing seasons are long.

If you live in an area with very sandy soil, you'll have to water more frequently. This means you'll also have to add nitrogen more often, since frequent watering leaches it from the soil. In such areas, you can keep your annuals growing vigorously by applying liquid nutrients at quarter to half strength with each watering.

A Fertilizer Primer

Most commercial fertilizers are "complete," meaning they contain the three major plant nutrients: nitrogen (N), phosphorus (P), and potassium (K). The percentage of each nutrient is given on the package label; an 8-5-5 contains by volume 8 percent N, 5 percent P, and 5 percent K. For best performance and bloom, a plant needs all three of these nutrients.

Checking the percentages of nutrients (particularly nitrogen) by volume in a container of fertilizer gives you a basis for comparing prices. For example, a 10-pound bag of 10-5-5 fertilizer contains half the nitrogen of a same-size bag of 20-5-5. With all else being equal, the 10-5-5 product should be worth half as much.

Nitrogen is the most important nutrient, used to form proteins, chlorophyll, and enzymes necessary for normal cell function and reproduction. If a plant receives too little nitrogen, leaves turn yellow and growth is stunted. An excess, on the other hand, produces rank, sappy growth vulnerable to insects and disease, and may reduce the number of flowers.

Nitrogen is useful to plants only in its nitrate form; if applied in its organic or ammonium form, the element must be converted to nitrate in the soil before roots can absorb it. But nitrates are water soluble, easily leached beyond the reach of roots. For this reason, plants require nitrogen in greater quantity than phosphorus or potassium, which remain available to plants once they are applied.

Plants use *phosphorus* to form nucleic acids important for early growth and for root and seed formation.

Unlike nitrogen, phosphorus is not water soluble. Instead, it binds chemically to mineral particles in the soil and is then taken up by the roots. It must be applied where the roots are (or where they are to be): dig it into the soil or apply it in deep trenches. If you spread it on the soil surface, it will bind to particles in only the top inch or two of soil—and so will be assimilated by only the shallowest roots.

Potassium helps transport sugars and starches and is necessary for root growth, disease resistance, and fruiting. The water-soluble potassium in fertilizers goes through an intermediate step in the soil to become *exchangeable potassium*, which roots can absorb by contact. Potassium should also be applied at root level.

Maintaining Appearance

Once you have prepared the soil, planted, fertilized, and maintained soil moisture, most of the work is done. There are, however, a few additional practices that can keep your annuals looking their best.

Weeding. Keep weeds pulled or hoed from the very beginning. They rob desirable plants of water and nutrients while making your flower bed look unkempt.

If you are planting large areas or are bothered by particularly troublesome weeds, you might want to consider using an herbicide. *Pre-emergent* herbicides kill weed seeds before they germinate. They can be sprayed over or worked into the soil before or after planting. *Post-emergent* (or contact) herbicides affect growing weeds.

Pinching. Most annuals are bred to be compact and well branched. However, some, including petunias, geraniums, and many chrysanthemums, benefit from pinching (see illustration at right) to promote bushiness. Others, including marigolds and zinnias, will produce better overall bloom if you pinch out the first blossoms that form on young plants. In general, pinching any plant that has become too leggy or too tall will make it bushier and more compact.

Staking. If a plant starts to fall over or becomes too leggy when in bloom, it needs to be staked. Staking is usually necessary only with the tallest annuals, or ones that are not getting enough sun. The illustration at right shows some common methods. The important thing is to support the flowers while concealing the stakes.

Deadheading. Once flowers have faded, a plant puts its energy into ripening its seeds so it can reproduce. This is usually done at the expense of new flower production. In other words, a plant that is ripening seeds produces less bloom.

Removing spent flowers, called deadheading, can do more than keep a garden looking neat; it can prolong bloom. Large-flowered annuals, such as zinnias, are easy to deadhead: just pinch off or cut flowers back to the next branch. With smaller-flowered plants, such as alyssum and verbena, it's easier to shear the flower heads off with pruning shears. Make sure you don't cut back too far: never remove more than a third of the plant. Follow up with a feeding.

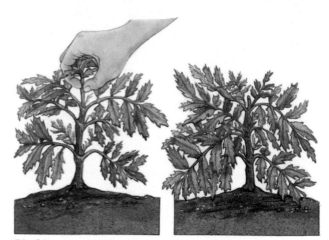
Pinching promotes bushiness and more bloom.

Staking keeps tall or leggy plants from falling over.

Deadheading encourages a longer bloom period.

Container Gardening

Gardening in containers and hanging baskets seems to become more popular every year. Particularly with annuals, container gardening lets you bring the flowers into close visual range, where they can really be enjoyed, on patios and decks and in entryways. There is a wealth of handsome containers to choose from. Whether you prefer a rustic oak half-barrel or a stylish ceramic pot, the only requirement is that the container have holes in the bottom for drainage.

On pages 24 to 25 is a list of plants that are ideally suited for growing in containers; on page 26 is a similar list of plants for use in hanging baskets. But before you jump in, realize that some of the basic rules for growing annuals change slightly when you switch to containers.

Soil. Choose a lightweight, sterile potting soil specifically designed for container gardening. A good mixture provides just the right balance of drainage, aeration, and moisture-holding capacity for ideal root growth. Potting soils are sold in bags at nurseries and garden centers, and in bulk from companies that sell topsoil.

If you have a lot of pots to fill, you may want to mix your own potting soil, although thoroughly blending one is quite a bit of work. One of the easier soil formulas calls for mixing ⅔ cubic yard nitrogen-stabilized bark (or peat moss) with ⅓ cubic yard washed 20-grit sand and adding to this 6 pounds of 0-10-10 dry fertilizer and 10 pounds of dolomite or dolomitic limestone.

Don't use ordinary garden soil in containers. No matter how good it is, the results are rarely as pleasing as with potting soil.

Watering. Soil in containers dries out very quickly, and you have to be vigilant in keeping it moist. In hot or windy weather, you might have to water more than once a day.

Inspect your containers often. If they feel light when you lift them, or if the top 2 inches of soil are dry, it's time to water. When you do water, apply enough to wet the entire rootball—enough so that some water runs out the bottom of the pot. This may take several passes with a hose.

If the rootball is really dry, it may shrink away from the edges of the pot, making it very difficult to wet. If water keeps running down the space along the edges, you may have to partially submerge the pot in a tub so it can absorb water from the bottom.

There are two ways you can ease container watering chores. The first is to mix super-absorbent soil polymers in your potting soil. Available in most nurseries, these hold hundreds of times their weight in water, which is still available to irrigate plant roots. Adding polymers to the potting soil lets you stretch the intervals between waterings.

A drip-irrigation system can also go a long way toward easing watering chores, especially when used with an automatic timer. Your local nursery or irrigation supply store can help design a system for containers.

Fertilizer. Potting soils may contain few nutrients, and any nitrogen they have is quickly leached out by watering. Consequently, container-grown annuals need frequent fertilizing. Liquid fertilizers are easiest to use. Start right after planting; repeat at least every 2 weeks.

Another alternative is to mix a timed-release fertilizer into the potting soil before planting.

Hanging Baskets

Growing annuals in hanging baskets is very similar to growing them in containers. The only difference is that hanging baskets, being exposed to the elements on all sides, dry out faster. Unless you are willing to water twice a day in hot weather, install an automatic drip system to keep baskets moist.

Instructions for building and planting a moss-lined hanging basket are illustrated below. Many nurseries carry moss baskets as well as a variety of hanging baskets made of wood, plastic, and clay.

Line the metal frame generously with moist sphagnum moss. Push moss firmly between wires. Plant sides: using your finger, make holes in the sides of the basket and insert each annual. Fill basket with soil. Plant top.

Pests & Diseases

The best way to reduce the chances of pest and disease problems is to keep your garden clean; plant well-adapted species and varieties (resistant to common pests, if possible); and provide the appropriate amounts of light, water, and fertilizer. If pests do strike, take prompt action to thwart them. If disease appears, treat it promptly or remove and destroy affected plants and plant parts.

Below, we list the most common pests and diseases that may affect annuals and suggest some controls and preventative measures. Try physical and biological controls first; if those fail, use packaged controls.

Aphids. Soft, rounded, and up to matchhead-size, aphids may be green, pink to reddish brown, or black. They cluster on new growth, sucking plant juices. Heavy infestations can devitalize a plant, distort growth, and aid in the spread of viruses.

Controls. Aphids are easy to dispatch with a strong spray of water or insecticidal soap. There are also many predators of aphids, including lacewing larvae and ladybird beetles. Or spray with pyrethrins, rotenone, diazinon, or malathion.

Beetles. In this category are various hard-shelled insects that chew holes in foliage and flowers. Grubs (small worms), the larval stage, live in soil. Japanese beetles (see photo) and cucumber or diabrotica beetles (¼ inch, yellow with black spots) are very destructive.

Control. Hand-pick and destroy beetles. Use the biological control, milky spore, for Japanese beetle grubs or hormone traps for adults. Malathion and Sevin are effective chemical controls.

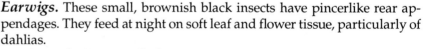

Earwigs. These small, brownish black insects have pincerlike rear appendages. They feed at night on soft leaf and flower tissue, particularly of dahlias.

Controls. Leave rolled, moist newspaper in the garden at night. Earwigs will hide in it in the morning. They can then be disposed of in a bucket of water. Or use earwig baits containing Baygon or Sevin.

Geranium budworms. Larvae of night-flying moths, they attack geraniums, ageratum, nicotiana, and petunias, rendering them bloomless. The small caterpillar eats the unopened buds or flowers, taking on the color of the flower on which it feeds.

Controls. If you see a bud with a small hole in it, pick and step on it or destroy it. That will kill the small larvae. For heavy infestations, spray with the biological control, *Bacillus thuringiensis*, or use pyrethrins, Sevin, or Orthene.

Mites. Tiny spiders appear as specks of red, yellow, or green dust and form silvery webs on the undersides of leaves.

    Controls. Frequent sprays with a strong jet of water will help dislodge them. Adding insecticidal soap to the water is even more effective. Natural predators include lacewing larvae and several species of predatory mites. Kelthane is the most effective chemical control.

Slugs, snails. These destructive garden pests are very common. They feed at night and on cool, overcast days; on warm sunny days, they hide. Both creatures eat leaves.

    Controls. Hand-pick and destroy any you can find. Or place boards out at night, turn them each morning, and crush the pests. They are also attracted to the fermented yeast in beer: place a beer-filled tray in the garden at night, and many will drown in it. There are also copper and salt-impregnated barriers that can be placed around beds. Or use baits containing metaldehyde or mesurol.

Whiteflies. These tiny, white, flying pests feed on undersides of leaves. Nymphs suck plant juices.

    Controls. Spray plants with insecticidal soap or use yellow, sticky traps. There are many natural enemies, including parasitic wasps. Dursban is an effective chemical spray.

Powdery mildew. A white or grayish powdery or mealy coating appears on leaves and flower buds, especially on dahlias and zinnias late in the year.

    Controls. Once established, powdery mildew is difficult to control. It's best to remove and discard infected plants. Benomyl and triforine are preventative sprays with some chance of success if you spray at the first signs of infection.

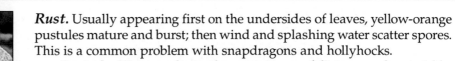

Rust. Usually appearing first on the undersides of leaves, yellow-orange pustules mature and burst; then wind and splashing water scatter spores. This is a common problem with snapdragons and hollyhocks.

    Controls. Water early in the morning so foliage can dry quickly. Avoid overhead watering. Give your planting area a good winter cleanup. Triforine, chlorathalonil, and wettable sulfur are effective preventative sprays. If an infestation occurs, remove and destroy infected plants or plant parts.

Annuals A to Z

In the following 41 pages, you'll find descriptive profiles of more than 100 flowering annuals. Some, such as marigolds (Tagetes) and zinnias, have been old standbys for decades and can be found in almost any mail-order catalog or retail nursery. Others, such as Dahlberg daisy (Dyssodia) and twinspur (Diascia), are relatively new to American gardens and deserve to be more widely planted. These may be slightly harder to find in nurseries, but are available by mail: see page 94 for catalog sources.

Viola

Bright yellow marigolds (Tagetes) and creeping zinnia (Sanvitalia) edge pinkish red petunias.

Using Our Encyclopedia

Our encyclopedia lists the annuals by their botanical names, the most reliable nomenclature. Each Latin name is followed by a common name (or names) and the identity of plant family to which that annual belongs. If you're looking for a plant and only know its common name, refer to the index on pages 95–96.

The information provided on each annual is designed to help you evaluate its suitability to your garden, and to help you grow it successfully. Each entry begins with a thumbnail sketch covering the plant's primary season of bloom, its range of flower colors, the exposure (sun or shade) in which it does best, its height, and the best time to plant. Planting time, indicated by season, assumes you use the most reliable method to start the plants: sowing seeds indoors or outside, or transplanting seedlings purchased at a nursery. However, unless otherwise noted, almost any annual that can be grown from seed can also be started from nursery transplants, if available. Exact planting dates for your region are best determined by checking average frost dates (see page 39).

Following this information is a description of the plant and its flowers, an indication of which varieties are most commonly available, and tips for using it most effectively in a particular site or design.

Finally, each encyclopedia entry gives you the cultural information you need to grow the plant successfully from seed to bloom.

Abelmoschus moschatus

ABELMOSCHUS MOSCHATUS
Silk flower
Malvaceae

Flowers in: Summer to frost
Colors: Red or pink with white centers
Exposure: Full sun
Grows to: 12 to 15 inches
When to plant: Sow seeds outdoors after all danger of frost is past

A relative of okra, silk flower produces abundant five-petaled, 3- to 4½-inch-wide, single flowers resembling tropical hibiscus. It is a bushy plant about 12 to 15 inches tall and as wide, with deep green, deeply divided leaves. It is most floriferous in areas with long, hot summers. Silk flower grows best in good garden soil, heat, and full sun, but will also bloom in partial shade. Flowering 100 days after sowing, it will continue to bloom up to frost or cold weather. It can be grown indoors in a window with bright light. 'Mischief' and 'Mischief Soft Pink' are vigorous hybrids.

Culture. Soak seeds in tepid water for 1 hour before sowing. Plant outdoors, covering the seeds lightly, as soon as the ground is warm. Or start indoors 6 to 8 weeks before transplanting outdoors. Germination takes place in 10 to 14 days. Water regularly.

AGERATUM HOUSTONIANUM
Floss flower
Compositae

Flowers in: Early summer to fall
Colors: Azure blue, lavender blue, white, pink
Exposure: Sun, or filtered shade in hot climates
Grows to: 12 to 26 inches
When to plant: Set out transplants in spring after all danger of frost is past; in mild-winter climates, set out transplants in late summer for fall bloom

Ageratum, originally from Mexico, is a reliable favorite for summer and fall color. Mound-shaped plants produce showy, fluffy blossoms, which offer

Ageratum houstonianum

one of the truest blues in the garden. The tiny tassel-like flowers are borne in dense clusters. Leaves are roundish (usually heart-shaped at the base), dark green, and hairy.

Dwarf varieties such as 'Blue Puffs' and 'Blue Blazer' are attractive upright plants, excellent for edging, bedding, or containers and for mixing with other low-growing annuals such as sweet alyssum, dwarf marigolds, and petunias. Taller varieties are more open in growth and are excellent as cut flowers, lasting a long time in water. 'Blue Horizon', which grows 30 inches high, is one of the most widely available. 'Capri' is a dynamic bicolor of mid-blue with contrasting white centers, growing 12 to 15 inches tall.

Culture. Plant in full sun except in hot-summer climates, where filtered shade is better. Be sure soil is warm before transplanting outdoors. Rich moist soil is ideal, although average soil is adequate provided plants are kept watered. In mild-winter areas, plant in late summer for fall color.

Ageratum is most conveniently grown from purchased transplants. Young plants are tender and slow to develop, but are easy to transplant, even when in bloom. Pinch back after planting out to promote bushiness. Space dwarf varieties 6 inches apart, tall ones 12 to 18 inches. Deadheading helps keep plants looking neat and promotes continued flowering. *Ageratum* is not frost tolerant; the first frost will kill the plants.

Seeds germinate in 5 to 10 days at 60° to 70°F/16° to 21°C and take 6 to 10 weeks to reach transplant size.

Alcea rosea

ALCEA ROSEA (ALTHAEA ROSEA)
Hollyhock
Malvaceae

Flowers in: Summer
Colors: White, pink, rose, red, purple, creamy yellow, apricot
Exposure: Full sun
Grows to: 6 to 8 feet; dwarf varieties to 36 to 40 inches
When to plant: Sow seeds indoors in winter to early spring for summer bloom

The stately bloom spikes of hollyhocks have adorned countless gates and doorways. This finest of background plants was originally a short-lived Chinese perennial. It is now generally grown as a biennial, although annual strains bloom the first year from seed if sown in early spring. With good luck, you will get a second year of bloom from the original plants, and the plants often self-seed. Hollyhocks are an old-fashioned favorite that look best against a fence or wall or at the back of a border. Old single varieties can reach 9 feet; newer strains are generally shorter. The erect plants are clothed in big, rough, heart-shaped leaves. Single, semidouble, or double saucer-shaped flowers that are 3 to 6 inches wide and sometimes have frilly edges bloom on spikes from the bottom upward.

Summer Carnival, with double blooms in a wide range of colors, will flower the same summer from spring sowing. Powderpuff has fluffy, 4-inch double blooms on dwarf 4- to 5-foot plants.

Culture. Start seed in January or February in mild-winter areas, in March in other climates, sowing at a depth of ⅛ inch. Germination takes place in about 9 days at 55°F/13°C. Set out plants, or sow seeds directly, in ordinary garden soil as soon as warm weather has arrived. Direct-seeded plants may not bloom until the following year. Set plants 18 to 24 inches apart. Water well. If the site is windy, hollyhocks need staking. Japanese beetles particularly like the leaves of hollyhocks. Rust and anthracnose are common diseases.

AMARANTHUS
Love-lies-bleeding, Summer poinsettia
Amaranthaceae

Flowers in: Summer to frost
Colors: Brilliantly colored foliage ranges from chocolate brown to crimson, bright green, and gold
Exposure: Full sun or partial shade
Grows to: Taller varieties to 4 feet; smaller varieties to 24 inches
When to plant: Sow seeds outdoors in late spring to early summer

Amaranthus are easily grown and a good choice for backgrounds, borders, or to create a point of interest. Although they are coarse, sometimes weedy plants, a few choice cultivars exhibit brilliantly colored foliage or flower spikes, commanding attention from midsummer until frost.

A. tricolor 'Illumination' has heavy stalks of pendant foliage forming a wide 4-foot column, the upper third of which is crimson crowned with gold. The popular Joseph's Coat is 24 inches tall, bearing multicolored foliage of yellow, green, and crimson, with lance-shaped leaves. *A. caudatus*, love lies bleeding, has erect or cascading spikes of green or shades of red; these can be air-dried for winter bouquets.

Picked when young and tender, the leaves and stems of many species can be cooked like spinach.

Culture. Sow seed outdoors in average garden soil in full sun or part shade after the soil has warmed. Germination usually takes 14 to 21 days. Space smaller varieties 18 inches apart, taller ones 24 to 36 inches.

Amaranthus

Ammi majus

AMMI MAJUS
White lace flower, Bishop's flower
Umbelliferae

Flowers in: Summer
Colors: White
Exposure: Full sun
Grows to: 34 to 36 inches
When to plant: Sow seeds outdoors in early spring

The round, flat, 5- to 6-inch flower heads of *Ammi majus* look like Queen Anne's lace, but the plants are not as weedy or invasive. The pure white color and airy habit are welcome in borders. Easy to grow and free-flowering, *A. majus* is excellent for cutting.

Culture. This plant resents transplanting; sow seeds where they are to grow. Seeds germinate in 7 to 14 days.

Ammobium alatum

AMMOBIUM ALATUM
Winged everlasting
Compositae

Flowers in: Summer
Colors: Silvery white with yellow centers
Exposure: Full sun
Grows to: 12 to 36 inches
When to plant: Sow seeds outdoors in early spring or in fall in mild-winter climates

Winged everlasting is a half-hardy perennial originally from Australia, now commonly grown as an annual in North America. It is prized for its faintly spicy flowers with glistening silvery white petals and yellow centers. The long, oval, woolly leaves grow in a clump at the base of the plant. The blossoms do not fade with age, making winged everlasting extremely useful in dried arrangements. Its common name refers to the stems, which are stiff, branched, and have raised ridges or "wings."

Culture. Sow seeds outdoors (sandy soil is best) ¼ inch deep as soon as the ground can be worked. In mild climates, seeds may be sown in fall. Plant in full sun, thinning to stand 10 to 15 inches apart. For earlier bloom, start seeds indoors 6 to 8 weeks before last frost and transplant outdoors after all danger of frost is past.

Plants often self-sow. For dried arrangements, cut when the flowers are past bud stage but not fully open. It is best to pick them on a dry, sunny day. Hang them upside down in a shaded, well-ventilated place to dry.

ANCHUSA CAPENSIS
Summer forget-me-not, Bugloss, Cape forget-me-not
Boraginaceae

Flowers in: Summer
Colors: Blue
Exposure: Full sun
Grows to: 9 to 19 inches
When to plant: Start seeds indoors 6 to 8 weeks before last frost; set out plants in spring, after all danger of frost is past

The rich blue, white-centered, somewhat tubular flowers of summer forget-me-not contrast splendidly with the reds and yellows so prevalent among summer-flowering annuals. Flowers are red in bud, ultimately blue, ¼ inch wide, and clustered on hairy, branching stems. Leaves are bright green and lance-shaped. *Anchusa* is good for edging, or try massing it in beds or borders to dramatize the vivid blue color. It combines particularly well with yellow marigolds and red petunias.

'Blue Angel' is a free-flowering, compact plant (to 9 inches) with intense ultramarine flowers.

Culture. Plants grow readily in any well-drained soil in full sun. Chill seeds 1 week before sowing. Sow ⅛ inch deep. Maintain night temperatures of 70°F/21°C and daytime temperatures of 85°F/29°C; germination takes about 14 to 21 days. Transplant seedlings outdoors 6 to 12 inches apart, and keep them well watered. After the first flush of bloom, cut plants back to within 6 to 8 inches of the ground;

Anchusa capensis

Annual grasses

they will rejuvenate quickly and be more beautiful than ever. Fertilize lightly if at all.

ANNUAL GRASSES
Gramineae

Flowers in: Spring to fall
Colors: Green, silver, gold, plum
Exposure: Sun
Grows to: 12 to 36 inches, depending on variety
When to plant: Sow seeds indoors in late winter in short-season areas, outdoors in early spring elsewhere

Plum-hued, waving grasses; silvery, slender grasses; tall, majestic grasses—all of these deserve a spot in a garden. Grown for their seed heads rather than their leaves, annual grasses lend a charming mistiness when interplanted with flowers. Low sorts are excellent for bordering tall plants that look better with their bases covered. Taller types add a vertical elegance or create a focal point. Annual grasses are also wonderful mixed with flowers in containers. Some grasses are useful to cut for winter bouquets, and others are attractive planted in beds by themselves.

There are many species to choose from. Cloud grass, *Agrostis nebulosa*, is a fine, hairlike grass, giving a hazy effect. Growing 18 inches tall, it blooms in early summer and then dies back. Quaking or rattlesnake grass comes in two forms: *Briza maxima* grows 18 inches tall, while *B. minor gracilis* is shorter, reaching a height of about 12 inches. Both have flat, drooping, oval or heart-shaped spikelets that dangle from wiry stems and resemble rattle-snake rattles. Quaking grass is best used in a cutting garden, as it is a bit ungainly for more tailored borders. It also dies back after "blooming" in early summer. Brome grass, *Bromus brizaeformis*, is similar to quaking grass but grows taller, to a height of 24 inches. Job's grass, *Coix lacryma-jobi*, grows 24 to 36 inches high and produces curious pearly gray seeds that hang from leaflike sheaths. It will do best in a moist spot in the garden. Each seed is about the size of a cherry pit, and is hard.

Love grass, *Eragrostis interrupta*, closely resembles cloud grass when planted in masses. Spikelets are small and dancing. Squirrel-tail grass, *Hordeum jubatum*, is of interest because of its short, feathery heads of bloom, which reach 24 to 36 inches high. Hare's-tail grass, *Lagurus ovatus*, is a short-growing plant with downy white 1- to 1½-inch-long tufts at the tips of the stems. It is useful as a low edging for other annuals and grows 12 to 18 inches tall. It is also long-lasting in winter bouquets because the flower heads will not shatter with age. *Zea*, or striped maize, can be attractive in bold masses. Its green leaves are striped with yellow, white, red, or pink. It grows 24 to 36 inches high and should be planted at the same time as corn. Striped maize is attractive planted in medium-sized pots and grouped on a patio or terrace.

Culture. In general, the annual grasses are easy to grow. Most grow quickly, and should be sown outdoors in early spring or started indoors 6 weeks earlier in areas with shorter growing seasons. In mild-winter climates, most can be sown outdoors in fall or winter. One of the trickier aspects of growing annual grasses is that, until they bloom, they look like grassy weeds. Label them carefully so you don't pull them out by mistake.

A way to avoid having flower beds that look as though they are full of weeds is to sow annual grasses seeds in 6-inch pots or flats. Once the grasses have come up and have nicely filled in, knock them from the containers, cut the root mass into small pieces (like lawn plugs), and transplant them into the garden.

Grasses require room to develop. Plant them at least 12 inches apart. The smaller grasses look better when planted in substantial drifts of the same species. Seed can be collected for following seasons.

To gather for winter bouquets, pick grass with flowers that have not yet opened completely, cutting the stems as long as you can. Strip excess leaves, tie stems together, and hang upside down in a cool, dry, airy room. They should air-dry in 2 to 3 weeks.

ANTIRRHINUM MAJUS
Snapdragon
Scrophulariaceae

Flowers in: Winter to spring in mild-winter climates, spring to summer in other areas
Colors: Reddish purple, lavender, crimson, red, white, yellow, bronze, orange, pink, and combinations
Exposure: Full sun
Grows to: Tall varieties to 36 inches; intermediate to 18 inches; dwarf to 12 inches
When to plant: Set out transplants in early spring in cold-winter climates, in fall in mild-winter areas

Snapdragons are fantastic in form and color, come in a great range of heights, and bloom abundantly. They are an excellent choice for sunny borders and cutting. The common name is easily understood by anyone who has pinched the throat of the flower and watched the hinged blossom open and close. Native to the Mediterranean region (in mild climates, they are perennials and bloom from early winter until summer), snapdragons are usually treated as annuals. They are available in three height ranges: tall, intermediate, and dwarf. Tall and intermediate forms provide colorful vertical accents. Dwarf kinds are useful for edgings, in pots, and in rock gardens. For most gardens, snapdragons of medium height are best, since they produce stems long enough for cutting but are not tall enough to require staking.

The flowers, to 1½ inches long, are borne in terminal racemes blooming from bottom to top. A single plant may produce 7 or 8 blossom spikes in the course of the season. Foliage is medium green, lance-shaped, and somewhat sticky.

Antirrhinum majus

Of the tall kinds, the Rocket and Madame Butterfly hybrids produce strong plants and magnificent flowers. Among intermediates, the Sonnet series produces a good color range, and the Liberty series has shapely spikes of large, brightly colored flowers. The dwarf Little Darling and Floral Carpet hybrids are vigorous and colorful. The Sweetheart series has double azalea-type flowers.

Culture. Snapdragons are most easily grown from purchased transplants, as seeds must be started indoors up to 3 months before setting out. If growing from seed, start in a coldframe or indoors where night temperatures are 45° to 50°F/7° to 10°C and day temperatures do not exceed 65°F/18°C. Seeds germinate in 1 to 2 weeks. Young plants don't grow in hot weather. Keep plants in vigorous growth, watering and feeding regularly. Avoid overhead watering, which can spread rust spores, but don't let plants dry out. It is advisable to change snapdragon planting locations from one year to another to discourage rust.

Space tall and intermediate plants 15 inches apart, dwarf plants 9 inches apart. Pinch tips to encourage bushy growth and abundant flowering.

As the flowers mature, use them freely for bouquets. Cut flower stalks when half of the flowers are open, cutting to within 4 inches of the base of the plant. This will encourage the plants to produce additional stems that will bloom later in the season and will delay the onset of rust. Stake taller varieties when they have 4 or 5 sets of leaves.

ARCTOTIS
African daisy
Compositae

Flowers in: Spring into summer
Colors: White, yellow, orange, red, purple, pink, and bicolors
Exposure: Full sun
Grows to: 12 to 24 inches
When to plant: Sow seeds outdoors in early spring in cold-winter climates, in fall in mild-winter areas

These colorful, easy-to-grow annuals form a wonderful carpet of color when direct-sown. Showy daisylike flowers bearing a contrasting ring of color around the central eye are borne on slender stems. Elongated leaves are lobed, rough, and hairy or woolly. African daisy does especially well in coastal gardens. The flowers, which close at night and on cloudy days, are good for cutting, although they last only a few days in water.

Arctotis hybrids are most commonly available and grow 1 to 1½ feet tall. The 3-inch flowers come in white, pink, red, purplish, cream, yellow, and orange, usually with a dark ring around the nearly black eye spot. In mild climates, plants make growth in winter and early spring and bloom from spring into early summer, with scattered bloom later. They will self-sow, but tend to revert to orange. Plants may survive as perennials in mild climates, but bloom best in their first year.

A. stoechadifolia grandis is a bushy annual to 2½ feet with gray-green, slightly hairy leaves. The 3-inch-wide, satiny white daisies have a yellow ring

Arctotis

surrounding a deep steel-blue central eye, haloed with light yellow and tinted lavender-blue on the reverse.

Culture. Plant seeds outdoors as soon as the soil can be worked in spring; or, for early bloom, start indoors in winter, planting to a depth of ⅛ inch. Germination takes about 8 days. Thin to stand 10 to 12 inches apart in sandy soil. Flowering begins approximately 11 weeks after sowing. Avoid excessive use of fertilizers, especially those high in nitrogen. Full sun is essential. African daisies do best with minimal watering.

BEGONIA SEMPERFLORENS
Bedding begonia
Begoniaceae

Flowers in: Late spring, continuing until frost
Colors: Shades of red and pink, and white; leaves are bright green or bronzy red
Exposure: Partial sun to shade
Grows to: Most 6 to 12 inches, a few to 16 inches
When to plant: Set out transplants after all danger of frost is past

Bedding begonias (or wax or fibrous begonias, as they are sometimes called) are native to South America. They are a large group of hybrids and cultivars that grow 6 to 12 inches tall and bloom continuously outdoors in summer. The blooms grow close together, often covering the glossy bronzy red or green foliage. They are superb for window boxes, hanging baskets, beds, and borders, and can also be grown as house plants. Blossoms may be single or double; some have large flowers, some clusters of smaller blooms.

Bedding begonias can be lifted in fall and potted as house plants, where they will bloom indefinitely in a window with bright light. Cuttings started from house plants in spring root readily to provide specimens for the summer garden.

Pizzazz is a series of uniform, early-blooming, green-leafed plants that hold up well to weather. The Cocktail series features dwarf plants with bronze foliage and flowers in a wide range of colors.

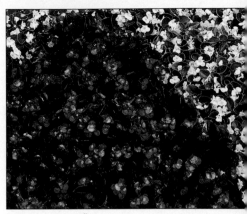

Begonia semperflorens

Culture. Since begonias take 12 to 16 weeks to grow from seed, it is much easier to start with nursery transplants. Set transplants outdoors in rich, moisture-retentive soil after all danger of frost is past. Provide shade from the afternoon sun, especially in hot climates, but avoid deep shade, which will make the plants grow leggy and set fewer flowers. Bronze-leafed varieties do better in full sun than the green-leafed ones. In fact, they darken with more light.

Seeds germinate in 2 to 3 weeks at 70° to 80°F/21° to 27°C and should be kept above 50°F/10°C at night.

BRACHYCOME IBERIDIFOLIA
Swan River daisy
Compositae

Flowers in: Spring into summer
Colors: Blue, pink, white
Exposure: Full sun
Grows to: 9 to 12 inches high and 12 inches wide
When to plant: Sow seeds outdoors after all danger of frost is past

Covered with a profusion of delicately fragrant blue, pink, or white flowers with dark eyes, Swan River daisies are excellent for massing in mixed beds and borders. Their soft hues are good complements to warmer-colored annuals like zinnias and marigolds. However, they are best adapted to cool-summer areas and burn out quickly in warm weather. Leaves are small and delicate, toothed, and dark green. The plant grows in a bushy, mounded habit

Brachycome iberidifolia

Brassica

that is suitable for growing in containers and hanging baskets.

Flowers may be cut for use in small vases, where they combine daintily with sweet alyssum. Use in rock gardens, as an edging, or in raised beds.

Culture. Sow seeds directly in ordinary garden soil, covering lightly; or, for earliest bloom, sow indoors in early spring. Germination takes about 8 days. Pinch the plants at 2 inches to induce bushiness. Thin to stand 5 to 6 inches apart. Flowering begins about 13 weeks after sowing and continues for 6 weeks or more in cool weather. Successive sowings result in a longer bloom period. The plants are fragile. Place short, brushy twigs among them to keep them from being beaten down by weather.

BRASSICA
Flowering cabbage & kale
Cruciferae

Flowers in: Early spring and fall, into winter in mild-winter climates
Colors: Grown for colorful foliage: green or white leaves with white, pink, rose, or purple markings
Exposure: Full sun
Grows to: 12 to 18 inches
When to plant: Best when started in mid to late summer to mature in the fall, since plants are most colorful in cool weather

Flowering cabbage and kale are excellent cool-weather bedding plants, providing magnificent rich foliage color late in the season. Looking a lot like their edible cousins, but without form-

ing tight heads, they yield textured rosettes of coarse foliage. Outer leaves are mostly smooth, often bluish green. The inner leaves are either off-white or deeply tinged with pink, rose, red, or purple, with color intensifying toward the center.

Flowering kale differs from flowering cabbage by being slightly looser in the head and more heavily fringed at the leaf edges. Cabbage forms lower-growing, flattened plants with broad heads.

Ornamental cabbage and kale produce a solid mass of color when planted as an edging or in a bed. They also grow well in containers and combine wonderfully with other fall and winter flowers, such as chrysanthemums and pansies. Their colored leaves set off gold and russet shades in fall arrangements. The foliage is also edible, though usually bitter-tasting, and makes a stunning garnish for all sorts of salads.

Culture. Plants are very similar to their edible cousins. When seed is started in midsummer and transplants are set out in late summer, heads mature beautifully in the cool months of fall. Colors actually intensify with light frosts. In mild-winter climates, plants will look good into winter. When planted in spring, ornamental cabbage and kale form looser heads and tend to bolt quickly as weather warms.

Start seeds 6 to 8 weeks before transplanting outdoors. Seeds germinate in about 10 days at 65° to 70°F/18° to 21°C. Space plants 15 to 18 inches apart in full sun. Protect seedlings from cabbage worms and aphids.

BROWALLIA SPECIOSA
Lovely browallia, Amethyst flower
Solanaceae

Flowers in: Late spring through summer
Colors: Blue, violet, and white
Exposure: Partial shade
Grows to: 12 to 36 inches
When to plant: Sow seeds indoors 8 to 10 weeks before last frost

Browallia produces a neat mound-shaped plant covered with brilliant blue, violet, or white flowers related to, and resembling, small petunias. Blue-flowering types have a contrasting white eye or throat. The one-sided clusters of velvety blooms are ½ to 2 inches long and as wide. *Browallia* blooms profusely for a long period in warm, moist, shady beds and borders. Where summers are short, it may not bloom until late summer or fall. Its leaves are lance-shaped, delicate, and bright green.

B. speciosa is most commonly grown. A sprawling plant with larger flowers to 2 inches in diameter, it lives over as a perennial in mild-winter climates. It is excellent for containers and hanging baskets because its mounding habit makes it drape over edges. 'Blue Bells Improved' is a compact variety with lavender blue flowers. 'Silver Bells' has pure white flowers and a trailing habit. The Troll series, including blue and white forms, produces compact, bushy plants well suited for growing in pots.

B. americana is branching, 1 to 2 feet high, with glossy roundish leaves; it is

Browallia speciosa

Bupleurum griffithii

... *Browallia speciosa*

easily grown and a pleasing border plant. Violet or blue tubular flowers ½ inch long and across are borne among leaves. 'Sapphire' is a free-flowering dwarf variety with dark blue flowers with white eyes.

Culture. Start *browallia* seeds indoors, uncovered, at 65°F/18°C, 8 to 10 weeks before the last frost. Germination takes 12 to 21 days. Plant 9 to 12 inches apart in fertile, evenly moist soil in partial shade. Fertilize regularly. Pinch frequently to promote bushiness and continued bloom. If cut back and potted up, *browallia* will bloom again indoors in winter.

BUPLEURUM GRIFFITHII
Umbelliferae

Flowers in: Summer
Colors: Yellow
Exposure: Sun or partial shade
Grows to: 12 to 18 inches
When to plant: Sow seeds indoors 6 to 8 weeks before last frost

This plant is enjoying new popularity in European floral markets as a filler for arrangements. *Bupleurum* has leaves like a eucalyptus and yellow flowers like a euphorbia. Its abundant fan-shaped branches provide a striking backdrop for any flower form or color. It's easy to grow and quickly yields lots of material for cutting.

Culture. Germination takes 20 days at 70°F/21°C. Plant out in ordinary soil in sun or partial shade. Water bupleurum regularly.

CALCEOLARIA
Slipper flower, Pocketbook plant
Scrophulariaceae

Flowers in: Spring to summer
Colors: Yellow, red, maroon, and pink—often with spots
Exposure: Partial shade
Grows to: 12 to 18 inches
When to plant: Set out plants in spring, after the danger of frost; in fall in mild-winter climates

Calceolarias are tropical American, tender perennials sometimes grown as half-hardy annuals. All have showy and interesting flowers with two lips. The upper lip is small and the lower one large, inflated, and slipperlike. They grow best outdoors in Western coastal areas or cool high-altitude gardens, as plants suffer in heat.

C. crenatiflora (C. herbeohybrida) is the species best known and usually called pocketbook plant. It grows 12 to 18 inches high and produces yellow, pink, red, and maroon flowers that often are speckled. It is usually grown by florists as an indoor pot plant and is difficult to grow from seed. The hybrid Anytime series is more heat tolerant. It does well in containers or planted in a mass outdoors.

Culture. It's easiest to start with nursery transplants, if you can find them. Otherwise, start seeds indoors 12 weeks before the last spring frost. In mild-winter areas, sow in midsummer for fall transplanting. Sow seeds, uncovered, at 70°F/21°C. After germina-

Calceolaria

Calendula officinalis

tion (in about 16 days), transplant to small pots and continue growing, with 50° to 60°F/10° to 16°C night temperatures. Plants grow best in moderately rich, slightly acid soil with regular watering. Cut back after flowering, and your plants may bloom again.

CALENDULA OFFICINALIS
Pot marigold
Compositae

Flowers in: Spring and early summer in cold-winter climates; fall through spring in mild-winter areas
Colors: White, cream, orange, yellow, and apricot shades
Exposure: Full sun
Grows to: 12 to 30 inches
When to plant: Sow seeds outdoors in early spring, in fall in mild-winter climates

Few annuals are easier to grow or flower more abundantly than these scentless Mediterranean natives. They have a bushy, upright habit and rich, harmonious flower colors. The 2- to 4-inch flowers are daisylike and range from white through cream and lemon to bright yellow, apricot, and orange. They bloom over a long period, provided faded flowers and seed heads are removed. Foliage is light green, hairy, and brittle. *Calendulas* are ideal for containers or as massed bedding plants, and are long-lasting cut flowers. The flower petals are edible, with a slightly tangy taste. Use fresh petals in salads, soups, and egg dishes; dried petals can be used all year in soups and rice.

Bon Bon, Fiesta, and Gypsy Festival strains offer dwarf plants 10 to 12 inches high with early bloom. The Princess series has black-centered flowers. Radio has quilled petals.

Culture. Calendulas thrive in full sun, rich soil, and cool weather. Sow seeds ½ to 1 inch deep as soon as the ground can be worked in spring. Or start seeds indoors 6 to 8 weeks before transplanting. Seeds germinate in 10 days. Thin or space plants to 12 to 15 inches apart. A second sowing in early summer gives a good autumn bloom. In mild-winter climates, sow again in late summer or early fall for winter and spring color. Protect plants from slugs and snails.

CALLISTEPHUS CHINENSIS
China aster
Compositae

Flowers in: Summer
Colors: White, creamy yellow, pink, red, blue, and lavender or purple (often with yellow centers)
Exposure: Full sun or light shade
Grows to: 6 to 30 inches
When to plant: Sow seeds outdoors in spring after all danger of frost is past

Asters are rather difficult to grow, since they dislike transplanting and are subject to several diseases. Still, they are treasured by gardeners for their brilliant colors and usefulness as cut flowers. Their botanical name is from the Greek, meaning "beautiful crown."

Callistephus chinensis

Asters are available in many different flower forms: daisylike, chrysanthemumlike, pincushion-type, peony-flowered, ball or quilled, curled, incurved, and with crested centers. They are branching, erect plants with hairy stems. Leaves are dark green and serrated or deeply lobed. Asters bloom for 4 to 7 weeks. You can extend their flowering season by planting early-, mid-, and late-season varieties or by planting successively through spring. In a border, they are outstanding massed in solid colors. Planting a mixture of colors provides a glowing rainbow in the garden.

Asters are unexcelled for cutting, with long stems and handsome foliage; a light, fresh scent; and a wide range of colors. And they are long-lasting. Unlike most annuals, asters quit blooming when they are cut. Whole plants can be dug up for indoor arrangements, as their branching habit makes each plant a bouquet in itself.

Pot 'n Patio is a dwarf series, to 6 inches, with double flowers available in single colors or a mixture, and is ideal for edgings and patio containers. It can also be grown indoors in a sunny window, and will bloom without supplemental light. The Matsumoto series offers medium-tall plants to 24 inches, bred for disease resistance and heat tolerance, featuring double flowers with yellow centers. Serene is a pompon version of Matsumoto. Seastar has large flowers with thin, curled petals, making a beautiful and unusual flower on 30-inch plants.

Culture. Asters are particularly susceptible to fusarium wilt, which causes young and old plants to turn yellow and wilt. Avoid the disease by planting wilt-resistant strains. Plant seeds outdoors, barely covering them, in rich, well-drained soil. Seeds germinate in 8 to 10 days. For a succession of bloom, start a few plants indoors several weeks before the last frost date. Space tall varieties 12 inches apart, dwarf varieties 6 to 8 inches. Stake tall kinds early. For show quality blooms, pinch out flowering shoots to allow 6 flowers per plant.

To avoid fusarium wilt, do not plant asters in the same bed year after year; and don't plant them in heavy clay

Campanula medium

soils, which tend to get waterlogged. Asters are also susceptible to the virus called aster yellows, carried by leafhoppers. Keep plants some distance from calendulas and remove nearby weeds, which can be hosts to insects and disease. Asters can be covered during the early part of the season with polyester row cover or cheesecloth to keep out disease-bearing insects. Remove and destroy plants infected with wilt or yellows.

CAMPANULA MEDIUM
Canterbury bells
Campanulaceae

Flowers in: Early summer
Colors: Predominantly blue, also pink, rose, lavender, and white
Exposure: Full sun in cooler climates; light shade in hot-summer areas
Grows to: 30 inches
When to plant: Set out transplants in early spring, in fall in mild-winter climates

Campanula is a large genus, the majority of which are biennials and perennials. The most common annual, *C. medium*, is originally a biennial, from which annual forms have been developed. Annual types are generally shorter, but the attractive, bell-shaped flowers are quite similar. The fine blue colors are particularly welcome in a border, and show off to advantage when fronted with colorful short-growing annuals such as Shirley poppies. The erect, pyramid-shaped spires of 2-inch-long flowers make unusual, long-lasting cut flowers.

(Continued on next page)

Capsicum annuum

. . . *Campanula medium*

Another member of the genus that is sometimes treated as an annual is *C. isophylla*. Plants in the F1 hybrid Stella series, offered in blue and white with 1-inch, star-shaped flowers and heart-shaped leaves, are excellent in containers. Planted in hanging baskets, they produce with their tidy habit a globe that is completely flower-covered all summer. Give them extra light, and you can force them to flower indoors in the winter.

Culture. Because plants take 6 months to flower from seed, transplants purchased from a nursery will provide earliest bloom. They transplant easily, even when in bloom. Space 12 inches apart in the garden. Plant in deep, moist loam or humus-enriched soil. Shade roots with other plants or mulch.

CAPSICUM ANNUUM
Ornamental pepper, Christmas pepper
Solanaceae

Flowers in: Summer
Colors: Yellow, orange, red fruits
Exposure: Full sun to partial shade, sunny window
Grows to: 8 to 10 inches
When to plant: Set out transplants after soil has warmed in spring

Ornamental pepper is unusual and decorative in the garden or in a container outdoors. The well-branched plants produce a mound of dark green leaves that are oval and pointed. Small white flowers are dainty and rather insignificant. The small round or cone-shaped peppers grow upright above the foliage and ripen from whitish green to yellow to orange and red. All of these colors are present at the same time as the individual ¾-inch fruits ripen. Ornamental peppers are good as an edging, mixed with marigolds or purple-leafed basil, or as a container or house plant. Grow outside during summer and bring indoors in the fall as an ornamental holiday plant.

'Holiday Cheer' is an All-America Selection with round fruit. 'Treasure Red' has tapered fruit.

Culture. Treat them like tomatoes and peppers, sowing seeds indoors at 75° to 80°F/24° to 27°C, 6 to 8 weeks before last frost; or purchase plants from a nursery. Seeds germinate in 5 to 8 days. Space plants 8 inches apart in average soil.

CARTHAMUS TINCTORIUS
Safflower, False saffron
Compositae

Flowers in: Summer
Color: Cream to orange shades
Exposure: Full sun
Grows to: 12 to 36 inches
When to plant: Sow seeds outdoors after all danger of frost is past

Carthamus, a native of Egypt, was once extensively cultivated for the yellow dye extracted from its flowers. Easily grown, the erect plants have serrated or spiny leaves (a spineless version is also available). The thistlelike 1½-inch-wide blooms are useful as cut flowers, fresh or dried. They provide a hard-

Carthamus tinctorius

Catharanthus roseus

to-find orange color for dried arrangements. The dried flower petals are sometimes used in place of true saffron, which they resemble in color and flavor (hence the common name).

Culture. Plant in average soil. Plants need little water, once established.

CATHARANTHUS ROSEUS (VINCA ROSEA)
Madagascar periwinkle
Apocynaceae

Flowers in: Late spring to fall
Colors: Shades of pink, rose, lavender, and white
Exposure: Full sun to light shade
Grows to: 20 inches
When to plant: Set out transplants after soil has warmed in spring

Catharanthus, often called annual vinca, is a veritable workhorse in a sunny garden. Erect, mounded plants or creeping, low-growing dwarfs are in constant bloom, producing single phloxlike flowers in harmonious colors. The glossy, dark green, oblong leaves complement the blooms nicely. Vinca is a free-flowering tender perennial grown as an annual. One of its greatest assets is that it blooms all summer. It is attractive edging a border, makes a lovely ground cover in a bed of lilies, and is graceful trailing from a window box. As easily grown as alyssum, it also self-sows. Pot up plants before the first frost and bring them indoors.

Among the upright vincas, the Cooler series, bred for cooler climates, offers earliest blooms and withstands summer heat. Its 7-inch plants bear large, brilliant flowers with overlapping, rounded petals. They are excellent in borders or in pots. 'Pretty-in-Pink', 'Pretty-in-Rose', and 'Pretty-in-White' are All-America Selections. Growing from 14 to 20 inches tall, they produce large flowers and create a colorful show throughout summer. The Carpet series of creeping periwinkles grows 3 inches tall, spreads 24 inches across, and provides color all season. These are beautiful cascading from hanging baskets.

Culture. Since seeds must be sown early indoors for earliest bloom, it's most convenient to start with transplants purchased at a nursery. Plant in average soil, 8 to 12 inches apart. Water and fertilize regularly to promote vigor. If growing from seeds, germinate at 78° to 80°F/26° to 27°C for 3 days, then 75° to 78°F/24° to 26°C for remainder of the 7- to 15-day germination period.

CELOSIA ARGENTEA
Cockscomb, Chinese woolflower
Amaranthaceae

Flowers in: Summer
Colors: Brilliant shades of yellow, orange, pink, red, and purple
Exposure: Full sun
Grows to: 12 to 36 inches
When to plant: Sow seeds outdoors in spring after the soil has warmed

Celosia is grown for its striking (sometimes considered grotesque) flower heads, which come in various forms. The flowers are vividly colored and so should be used with discretion. They are best massed together or planted near other brightly colored annuals. *C. argentea plumosa* has blossoms resembling ostrich plumes. The feathery stalks are an unusual formal accent and can be interesting in arrangements. *C. argentea cristata* has velvety, crested flowers that resemble the vivid combs of roosters. Both *celosias* have long, narrow, lance-shaped leaves that are often bronze-colored or have red margins. Dried, the colorful, dense flower heads make good additions to winter bouquets. Both varieties thrive in the heat of summer. Dwarf forms, especially the feathery ones, are useful in window boxes and containers. Place dwarf types in front of tall, branching varieties to create a colorful display.

Of the medium- to tall-growing celosias, the self-branching, 24-inch-high Century series of *C. a. plumosa*, available in single colors or a mixture, provides an early, colorful display. 'Century Red' is handsomely framed by bronze foliage, as is All-America Selection 'New Look', which grows 14 to 16 inches tall. Another award winner, 'Pink Castle', bears flowers of a beautiful rose-pink color on 12-inch by 12-inch plants. *C. a. cristata* 'Toreador' and 'Fireglow' feature intense red flower heads on 18- to 20-inch-tall plants.

In the dwarf range, *C. a. plumosa* Kimono offers an exciting mixture of uniform plumes in a broad range of colors on extra-dwarf 5- to 6-inch plants. *C. a. cristata* Jewel Box Mixture, to 5 inches tall, has large, comb-shaped blooms in a rich blend of colors; its neat, compact habit makes it ideal for bedding and containers.

Culture. Grow in rich garden soil. Plants respond well to feeding. They thrive in heat but not in cold, so do not sow or transplant too early. Keep the seedbed evenly moist, as seeds are sensitive to dry conditions. Seeds germinate in 8 to 10 days. Thin to stand 9 to 12 inches apart. In a nursery, look for young plants, as older transplants can suffer shock that inhibits flower production. To dry, cut the flowers and

Celosia argentea

Centaurea cyanus

hang them upside down in a dry, airy place. Strengthen *C. a. cristata's* stems with florist's wire to support the heavy flower heads.

CENTAUREA
Bachelor's button or Cornflower, Dusty miller, Sweet sultan
Compositae

Flowers in: Summer
Colors: *C. cyanus* and *C. moschata:* Blue, pink, rose, purple, yellow, and white; *C. cineraria* is grown for its silver foliage
Exposure: Full sun
Grows to: *C. cyanus* to 36 inches, *C. moschata* to 24 inches, *C. cineraria* to 12 inches
When to plant: Depends on variety (see below)

Centaurea is a diverse genus which includes the annuals commonly known as bachelor's button or cornflower, sweet sultan, and dusty miller.

C. cineraria is a silver-leafed plant called dusty miller—as are other silver-foliaged plants, such as the perennial *Senecio cineraria* and the annual *Chyrsanthemum ptarmiciflorum. C. cineraria's* felty, white, divided foliage makes it an elegant edging plant; the silver color softens and contrasts with bright flowers. It prefers relatively dry soil and tolerates heat, making it an excellent container plant. The cool hue of dusty miller complements hot-colored flowers such as geraniums, salvia, and petunias. It adds texture and interest in mixed plantings in window boxes or patio containers. It is also good foliage material for cut-flower arrangements. In mild-winter climates, it can be grown as a perennial and will send up 14- to 18-inch-tall stems of golden yellow blossoms in the spring. 'Silver Dust', 8 inches tall, has finely cut foliage and can be pruned to maintain a bushy shape.

C. cyanus is the popular bachelor's button or cornflower, a bushy plant with grayish, lance-shaped foliage and dense, thistlelike flower heads. It gives a lacy effect to a border and blooms prolifically, peaking in spring to midsummer. Excellent for cutting, its long-lasting, richly colored blossoms are unsurpassed in a summer bouquet. The traditional flower for boutonnieres, cut blossoms last for some time without water. Deadhead the old blooms to keep them in flower, or make successive sowings to prolong the bloom season. The plants self-sow, but the seedlings often revert to inferior flower forms. Birds are attracted to the seed heads. Try interplanting blue varieties with yellow- or orange-colored annuals such as California poppies or *Gazania*. Plant the tall and medium-tall varieties in the back or middle of a border. Dwarf forms are suitable for containers.

C. cyanus 'Blue Boy' has rich blue flowers and grows to 30 inches. Polka Dot Mixed is a charming dwarf, to 18 inches, with a bushy habit.

C. moschata, sweet sultan, has finely fringed, 3-inch-wide flowers with a delicate fragrance. It favors cool climates. 'The Bride', growing to 24 inches tall, has fragrant, pure white flowers that are excellent for cutting.

Culture. *C. cineraria* is slow-growing, and best purchased as transplants or started early indoors. Plant 8 to 9 inches apart outdoors after all danger of frost is past. *C. cyanus* is easily grown from seed; sow in the fall for the earliest possible start, or as soon as the ground can be worked in spring. Thin to 12 inches apart. Taller kinds should be staked. Sow seeds of *C. moschata* where they are to grow, as it resents transplanting. Thin to 8 to 12 inches apart. It's at its best in cool weather and must be planted in the garden in early spring to succeed. Flowering slows down in hot weather, but returns with cooler fall temperatures.

Cheiranthus cheiri

CHEIRANTHUS CHEIRI
Wallflower
Cruciferae

Flowers in: Spring or late summer
Color: Tones of yellow, orange, red, burgundy, purple, and brown
Exposure: Full sun or partial shade
Grows to: 12 to 24 inches
When to plant: Set out transplants in very early spring for spring bloom; for late-summer bloom, sow seeds outdoors in early spring. In mild-winter areas, sow seeds outdoors in fall

Wallflowers have long been cherished by gardeners in Britain, where the cool, damp climate favors them. They can be grown in this country in similar climates, such as the Pacific Northwest and the coastal Northeast, where they often live on as perennials. Wallflowers have showy, sweetly fragrant clusters of single or double flowers and an erect, bushy habit. Their 3-inch-long leaves are narrow and pointed. The richly colored ½- to 1-inch-wide blossoms make splendid cut flowers. Plant a few beneath a window or near a doorway so their sweet fragrance can waft through the house. They thrive along south-facing rock walls or foundations, where the soil and shelter suit them. Try planting them as companions for spring-blooming bulbs such as tulips.

Culture. Plant in moist soil with good drainage. Early-flowering varieties will bloom about 5 months after sowing. Seeds germinate in 5 to 21 days at a temperature of 54°F/12°C.

CHRYSANTHEMUM
Compositae

Flowers in: Spring, summer, and fall; winter in mild-winter climates
Colors: White and shades of yellow—some with red or purple zoning
Exposure: Full sun
Grows to: 4 to 24 inches
When to plant: Sow seeds outdoors or set out transplants in early spring, in fall in mild-winter climates

This important genus, usually thought of for its fall-blooming perennial varieties, includes several valuable annuals as well. All are excellent for spring and summer borders; many are incredibly free-flowering. They make fine, long-lasting cut flowers.

C. carinatum, tricolor chrysanthemum, is an erect, tall plant (up to 2 feet) with single or double ray flowers and a contrasting zone of purple, red, or yellow surrounding a dark purple eye. The foliage is deeply cut. 'Polar Star' is bright and charming, with white daisylike flowers and yellow zoning.

C. coronarium, crown daisy, is a bushy plant to 24 inches tall covered with 2-inch flowers, typically in shades of yellow. A native of southern Europe, it has pale green, deeply cut leaves. 'Primrose Gem' is a low-growing bush, 12 to 18 inches tall. Its flowers have golden centers set off by a double row of soft yellow petals.

C. multicaule and *C. paludosum*, mini-marguerites, are both small, well-branched annuals that prefer cool weather. They grow to 12 inches and

Chrysanthemum paludosum

produce masses of 1½-inch daisylike flowers, excellent for edging, window boxes, and hanging baskets. 'Yellow Buttons', just 4 to 7 inches tall, is a vigorous plant with bright yellow, single flowers. 'White Buttons', to 7 inches, is covered with flowers with white petals surrounding yellow centers.

C. ptarmiciflorum, silver lace (one of several plants known as dusty miller), has finely cut silver foliage and grows 8 inches tall.

Culture. Plant in average soil. Seeds germinate in 8 to 20 days at 68°F/ 20°C. Thin to stand 12 inches apart. Pinch young plants to promote bushiness. Plants do not tolerate heat well. Stake taller varieties. Remove spent blossoms to prolong bloom period.

CLARKIA
Onagraceae

Flowers in: Spring to early summer
Colors: Shades of white, yellow, red, pink, rose, and lavender
Exposure: Full sun
Grows to: 12 to 48 inches
When to plant: Sow seeds outdoors in early spring or in the fall in mild-winter areas

The clarkia family includes several beautiful Western wildflowers and hybrids. Natives of western North and South America, they were named for Captain William Clark of the Lewis and Clark expedition. Clarkias grow best in cool climates, thriving in mountainous areas of the West. They do not tolerate heat. Their showy flowers are attractive in borders or in beds. Clarkia stems are wiry and slender, and will be prostrate unless staked. They make good cut flowers, as they last several days in water.

C. amoena (*Godetia amoena*), commonly called godetia or farewell-to-spring, is a native of the west coast of North America. Its flowers grow in spikes above tapered, dark green leaves on 20- to 36-inch plants. Dwarf forms grow to 12 inches. The satiny single or double cup-shaped flowers are 2 inches across. In mild-winter climates, sow in fall for spring bloom.

C. concinna, red-ribbons, is native to California, and grows to 18 inches tall. The feathery pink-to-lavender flowers have deeply lobed petals, resembling ribbons. The bushy plant has small, oblong leaves.

C. pulchella grows to 15 inches tall. Single and double white, lavender, or carmine flowers are triple-lobed at the tips. The slender plant has reddish stems and narrow, pointed leaves. Single flowers are deeply toothed to a clawlike base. This clarkia works well near the front of a border.

C. unguiculata (*C. elegans*), clarkia or mountain garland, grows up to 4 feet tall. It is the most widely grown of the clarkias. Single or double 1- to 2-inch flowers grow in spikes above reddish stems and oval, lance-shaped leaves. The spring-blooming flowers, in scarlet, salmon, carmine, white, purple, rose, or creamy yellow, are effective massed. The frilly, double-flowered kinds are most widely available as seeds.

Culture. As clarkias do not like transplanting, sow seeds where they are to flower, in sandy soil without fertilizer. Soil needs to be cool (55°F/13°C) for germination, which can take from 5 to 20 days. Thin to stand 9 inches apart (space *C. unguiculata* 6 inches apart, as it blooms better when somewhat crowded). Keep soil moist until plants bloom.

Clarkia unguiculata

Cleome

CLEOME
Spider flower
Capparaceae

Flowers in: Summer to fall
Color: Shades of pink, purple, white, and yellow
Grows to: 5 feet
Exposure: Full sun or light shade
When to plant: Sow seeds outdoors after soil has warmed

An airy mass of *cleome* provides a colorful and unusual background at the back of a border. This plant (*C. spinosa*) can provide a quick-growing screen or hedge, and it blooms from summer until hard frost. Its bushy, somewhat coarse spikes are topped with clusters of single flowers. Stamens that are 2 to 3 inches long protrude from each flower, giving a distinctive airy effect. Long, narrow, pointed seed pods form below the flowers, like spider legs. The compound leaves are made up of leaflets arranged like fingers on a hand.

A member of the caper family, spider flower has a peculiar lemony odor that some find disagreeable. The plants tend to be leggy and leafless at the bottom, but this can be remedied by planting shorter-growing annuals in front of them. Thorns develop where flowering branches join the hairy main stem, so be careful when cutting for indoor bouquets. Cut flowers will continue opening for about a week indoors. Named varieties such as 'Helen Campbell' (white-flowered), 'Rose Queen', 'Ruby Queen', and 'Queen Mixed' display improved colors.

(Continued on next page)

Coleus hybridus

. . . Cleome

C. lutea is a Western wildflower with yellow flowers and pale green leaves.

Culture. This plant is easily grown from seed. Chill seeds overnight and plant in average soil. Seeds germinate in 10 to 14 days, growing best with 85°F/29°C days and 70°F/21°C nights. Space at least 24 inches apart. Stake to hold upright. Keep plants on the dry side to prevent them from getting leggy. Spider flowers self-sow and can become invasive.

COLEUS HYBRIDUS
Labiatae

Flowers in: Flowers insignificant
Colors: Foliage is green, chartreuse, yellow, buff, salmon, orange, red, purple, and brown—often with several colors on each leaf
Exposure: Filtered sun to light shade
Grows to: 24 inches
When to plant: Set out transplants in spring after the danger of frost

This Java native is grown for its vibrant, multicolored leaves. A member of the mint family, it has variegated coloring and toothed or ruffled foliage that can offer an uninterrupted display of color in a garden or container. *Coleus* is actually a tender perennial treated as an annual. It has small blue flower spikes, but these should be pinched out early to maintain the plant's bushy shape. A mass of coleus adds considerable color to a lightly shaded border. Placement makes a difference in coloration, as too much sun can bleach out foliage

color, while too much shade can also mute color.

The Wizard series has large, heart-shaped leaves and grows just 12 to 14 inches tall. The well-branched plants are superb in baskets and containers. Wizard is available in a wide range of color combinations. 'Volcano' grows to a similar size, with luminous scarlet leaves and a spreading habit. Among small-leafed kinds, Carefree offers a mixture of deeply lobed leaves on 10-inch bushy plants. Saber produces a mixture of long, vivid, saberlike leaves. Fiji is a fringe-leafed coleus that grows to 10 inches tall. 'Poncho Scarlet' has a cascading effect that is superb in hanging baskets. Its elongated stems hold broad, rainbow-type leaves of deep scarlet edged with chartreuse.

Culture. Coleus plants are easily grown from seeds, transplants, or cuttings. For garden use, start seeds indoors 10 weeks before the last frost. Seeds germinate in 10 days at 70° to 75°F/21° to 24°C, uncovered. Purchased seedlings from a nursery can offer an early start. Space plants 12 to 20 inches apart; pinch often to promote bushiness. Cuttings root easily in sand or water. In fall, make cuttings of the most attractive plants to use as house plants over the winter. Then make new cuttings in spring to plant outdoors.

CONSOLIDA AMBIGUA (DELPHINIUM AJACIS)
Larkspur, Annual delphinium
Ranunculaceae

Flowers in: Spring and early summer
Colors: White, blue, lilac, pink, rose, salmon, and carmine
Exposure: Partial shade
Grows to: 4 feet
When to plant: Sow seeds outdoors in fall or as soon as ground can be worked in spring

Prized because of its resemblance to the stately perennial delphinium and for its ease of culture, larkspur is indeed an asset to most flower gardens. Native to southern Europe, the upright plants have ferny, deeply cut foliage. Some forms of larkspur bear long, full, hyacinthlike spikes of blossoms with few side branches. Others

are well-branched and carry dense blossom clusters along their branches. Larkspurs provide excellent foliage and bloom for the middle and back of a border. Their pastel colors are set off to advantage against a dark background such as evergreens or a planting of *Perilla*. Dwarf varieties can provide intense color for the front of a border. The bloom season is rather short where summers are hot. Larkspurs are excellent for cutting.

'Dwarf Blue Butterfly' is a compact plant that grows to 14 inches tall, with 1½-inch-diameter flowers in a deep, intense blue. Giant Imperial produces upright 4-foot-tall plants with excellent-quality blue, carmine, lilac, pink, salmon, rose, and white blooms. The Dwarf Hyacinth Flowering series offers neat 12-inch-tall plants with spikes of tightly knit flowers in pink, violet, lilac, denim blue, and white.

Culture. Prepare a fertile, well-drained seedbed. Chill the seeds for 7 days to improve germination. Broadcast where plants are to grow (larkspurs resent transplanting) in late fall or very early spring. Lightly cover and tamp seeds in with the palm of your hand. Seeds germinate in 10 to 20 days. Provide plenty of moisture as the plants grow. Taller varieties benefit from staking.

Consolida ambigua

Convolvulus tricolor

CONVOLVULUS TRICOLOR
Dwarf morning glory
Convolvulaceae

Flowers in: Summer
Color: Blue, purple, lilac, red, pink, and white, with a band of white around the yellow throat
Exposure: Full sun
Grows to: 6 to 12 inches
When to plant: Sow seeds outdoors in spring after the soil has warmed; in short-growing-season areas, start seeds indoors 6 weeks before last frost

Convolvulus tricolor has 1½-inch-wide funnel-shaped blossoms, very similar to morning glory flowers. Like morning glory, this is a daytime bloomer, with the flowers closing at night. A native of southern Europe, it flowers continuously in dry, sunny locations, forming a neat mound up to 12 inches tall and with greater spread. It provides intense color and a good foundation at the base of taller plants and also excels in a rock garden. The mounding habit of dwarf morning glory makes it an excellent choice for containers, window boxes, and hanging baskets. 'Blue Ensign' has brilliant blue flowers on a compact, 6-inch-tall plant that spreads to 15 inches wide.

Culture. Nick each seed coat and soak seeds overnight in water before sowing. If sowing indoors, plant in peat pots to minimize root disturbance when transplanting. Germinate seeds at 60° to 65°F/16° to 18°C. The plant grows best in warm weather.

COREOPSIS TINCTORIA
Annual coreopsis, Calliopsis
Compositae

Flowers in: Summer
Colors: Yellow, orange, maroon, bronze, and shades of red, often with a contrasting band of color surrounding the purplish brown centers
Exposure: Full sun
Grows to: 24 inches
When to plant: Sow seed outdoors as soon as ground can be worked in early spring

Annual coreopsis has daisylike blooms that dance on the breeze above lacy, finely cut foliage. Its flowers are similar to those of perennial coreopsis. It resembles cosmos in growth habit. The plant is good massed in a sunny bed, as it tolerates heat. The common yellow form is pretty planted among cornflowers. Dwarf and double varieties are also available. It will bloom freely throughout summer, and often self-sows. The flowers are ideal for cutting.

Culture. Plant in average soil. Seeds germinate in 7 to 14 days. Space 6 to 8 inches apart, since plants bloom best when crowded. Stake taller varieties for support; their stems are wiry and slender.

Coreopsis tinctoria

Cosmos bipinnatus

COSMOS
Compositae

Flowers in: Late spring to early fall
Colors: Yellow, orange, red, white, pink, and bicolors
Exposure: Full sun to partial shade
Grows to: 24 inches to 7 feet
When to plant: Sow seeds outdoors in spring after any danger of frost

With its graceful flowers and airy, feathery foliage, cosmos is an invaluable addition to a border, and very easily grown. Its rapid growth and tall habit make it a good background for intermediate and dwarf annuals and perennials. Modern varieties are earlier-blooming than the original autumn-blooming Mexican natives. The serrated flower petals may be daisylike, or may be crested, doubled, or quilled around yellow centers. The graceful 1- to 2-inch-wide blossoms make excellent cut flowers, and the foliage can also serve well as a filler for bouquets.

  C. bipinnatus has flowers in white, pink, rose, lavender, purple, crimson, and bicolors. Make several successive sowings to assure a good supply of flowers, which will continue blooming until frost. The long, thin, branching stalks at the plant's base tend to look leggy, so set plants toward the back of a border, with short-growing annuals in front of them. Sensation is a bushy series with mixed blooms of rose, crimson, white, and pink; it blooms 10 weeks from seed. 'Imperial Pink' has single blooms of a deep rose-pink on strong, branching, 3- to 4-foot plants. 'Candystripe' has cool white

Crepis rubra

. . . Cosmos

flowers splashed with crimson. 'Sonata' offers snowy white flowers on plants only 24 inches tall.

C. sulphureus, yellow or Klondike cosmos, grows to 7 feet with bold yellow, golden orange, or scarlet-orange flowers. It can become weedy-looking, especially toward the end of the season. The Ladybird series provides free-flowering plants with semidouble blossoms on dwarf, compact, 12-inch plants. It is available in single colors of orange and yellow and as a mixture that includes scarlet. 'Sunny Red', an All-America Selection, has single scarlet flowers that soften to orange as they mature.

Culture. Sow seeds in well-drained average soil. Germination takes 5 to 7 days. Plants grow best in soil that is dry and not very fertile. Stake taller varieties to keep them upright. Space 12 inches apart. Remove spent flowers to keep plants blooming. Cosmos often self-sows.

CREPIS RUBRA
Hawk's beard
Compositae

Flowers in: Early summer
Colors: Pink, red, and white
Exposure: Full sun
Grows to: 15 to 18 inches
When to plant: Sow seeds outdoors in fall in mild-winter climates; elsewhere, sow as soon as ground can be worked in spring

This bushy Mediterranean native puts on a colorful show despite its small size. Slender flower stems rise above clumps of smooth, pale green, serrated or deeply lobed leaves. The 1½- to 2-inch-wide dandelionlike flowers are followed by clusters of soft, silvery hairs. The dried seed heads, if cut before they mature, can make a feathery addition to dried arrangements. The blossoms are not good for cutting, as they close in the afternoon. Hawk's beard is useful as an edging plant and handsome in a rock garden. 'Rubra' has pale pink to reddish flowers, while the cultivar 'Alba' has white flowers.

Culture. Seeds germinate in 10 days at 70°F/21°C. Hawk's beard thrives in poor soil. Thin plants to 4 inches apart.

CUPHEA IGNEA
Firecracker plant, Cigar plant
Lythraceae

Flowers in: Summer and fall
Color: Red
Exposure: Full sun or light shade
Grows to: 12 inches
When to plant: Set out transplants after soil has warmed in spring

Firecracker plant is a novelty, providing an unusual color accent in gardens or in containers. A native of Mexico, it has bright red ¾-inch-long tubular flowers, with black and white markings on the tip suggesting a burnt ash. Red is the most commonly available flower color, though some varieties have lavender, lilac, pink, or purple blossoms. The flowers grow on compact, bushy plants. The dark green, lance-shaped leaves are 1 to 1½ inches long and appear on reddish stems.

Cuphea ignea

Cynoglossum amabile

A tender perennial grown as an annual, firecracker plant prefers warm weather. It makes a colorful display when massed toward the front of a border. Or try it in containers mixed with the silvery foliage of dusty miller or variegated vinca. Cuttings are easily rooted in fall for use in indoor window gardens.

Culture. Firecracker plant flowers 4 to 5 months after sowing, so purchasing nursery-grown transplants is advantageous. Space plants 9 inches apart in average soil. Seeds germinate in 7 to 14 days at 68°F/20°C.

CYNOGLOSSUM AMABILE
Chinese forget-me-not
Boraginaceae

Flowers in: Spring to early summer
Colors: Blue, pink, and white
Exposure: Full sun to light shade
Grows to: 15 to 18 inches
When to plant: Start seeds indoors 4 weeks before last frost for earliest bloom, or sow seeds outdoors in early spring (in fall in mild-winter climates)

The fresh blue color of Chinese forget-me-not adds a cool accent among early-blooming warm-colored annuals such as orange *Dimorphotheca* and pink or rose *Dianthus*. The plant's habit is somewhat weedy. Its foliage is soft, hairy, and a grayish green. The ¼-inch-wide, star-shaped flowers are held in graceful tall sprays, most commonly of a deep or sky blue color.

The plant easily reseeds itself; in fact, volunteer seedlings can become a nuisance. The seeds cling to clothing and animal fur. 'Firmament' bears multitudes of sky blue flowers. 'Blue Showers' was bred especially to be used as cut flowers.

Culture. It's easily grown in average soil. Seeds germinate in 2 to 3 weeks at 68°F/20°C. Thin to stand 9 inches apart in groups of three or more plants. Deadhead to reduce the number of volunteer seedlings and promote flowering on side branches.

DAHLIA
Compositae

Flowers in: Summer to fall
Colors: Every color except blue
Exposure: Full sun for at least half the day
Grows to: 12 to 20 inches
When to plant: Sow seeds indoors 6 to 8 weeks before last frost, or purchase nursery-grown transplants for planting out in spring

Gardeners may be most familiar with the tall-growing tuberous dahlias that produce huge blossoms. Many are unaware that the smaller dwarf dahlias can be grown from seed as annuals that will, in the first year, produce a mass of bloom. Annual dahlias are actually tender perennials from Mexico. These early-flowering dwarf plants bloom profusely with brilliant 2- to 3-inch blossoms in many forms. Foliage is dark green or bronze. Plants look showy in a mixed border, and are ef-

Dahlia

fective massed together. Their vibrant display of color is almost unmatched by any other midsummer- or fall-blooming plant. Early-blooming 'Piccolo' produces single, 2½-inch, daisylike flowers on compact 8- to 10-inch plants, with a wide color range, including bicolors. The Figaro Improved and Sunny series offer 14- to 20-inch plants with double flowers, Figaro in mixed colors, Sunny in single colors of red or yellow. Extra-early Redskin has attractive bronze foliage with double flowers in mixed colors on 20-inch plants, and is an All-America Selection.

Culture. Seeds germinate in 10 to 20 days with daytime temperatures of 70° to 75°F/21° to 24°C. Plant in moist, fertile soil, spacing plants 24 to 30 inches apart. Over-fertilizing can promote foliage development at the expense of flowers. For larger, showier blossoms, pinch out side buds and leave only the buds at the top of the plant to bloom. Prune back lightly in midsummer to prolong the blooming season. Provide plenty of water during dry weather. As the plants are well-branched and sturdy, they do not usually require staking. Cut flowers will last longer if the cut stem ends are dipped into boiling water. Plants may winter over in mild-winter climates. Tubers can be dug and stored over the winter. It is best, however, to replace dwarf dahlias each year to assure vigorous bloom.

Earwigs are a common pest.

DIANTHUS
Pink, Carnation
Caryophyllaceae

Flowers in: Spring and summer
Colors: Shades of red and pink; also white, yellow, and mahogany
Exposure: Full sun
Grows to: 8 to 18 inches
When to plant: In mild-winter climates, sow seeds outdoors in fall. In other regions, start indoors at least 8 to 10 weeks before last frost

Dianthus is best known for its biennial and perennial species. Annual varieties are available in a number of flower forms and colors. The flowers have distinctive fringed or toothed petals,

Dianthus chinensis

and most are fragrant. The plants are equally successful in the ground or in containers. Dwarf forms are suitable for rock gardens.

D. caryophyllus is known as the hardy carnation. It is similar to florists' carnations, but has smaller blossoms and a spicier fragrance; the flowers add scent as well as color to arrangements. It is not hardy in cold-winter climates. The Knight series flowers within 5 months from seed, with strong, 12-inch stems supporting a continuous supply of blooms, available in shades of red, orange, yellow, and white. The blossoms are fragrant and the plant is heat tolerant. The Trailing Carnations Mix has a pendulous habit, and its pink and red blossoms bring a graceful cascade of color to window boxes and hanging baskets.

The China pink (*D. chinensis*) grows in clumps with single flowers borne atop strong, short stems. The faintly fragrant flowers are often splashed with contrasting colors. It is an excellent edging at the front of a border. 'Pink Flash' is very early-flowering, and the blooms lighten from mid-pink to pastel pink as they mature. The plants grow to 12 inches tall. Princess, a compact 8- to 10-inch-tall strain, blooms throughout summer. It is available in five colors. The Telstar series includes All-America Selection 'Telstar Picotee', producing crimson flowers with white fringes on 8- to 10-inch plants. The Parfait series is named for its festive layering of rich color. The 2-inch-wide flowers, borne in abundance, have an eye pattern of a deeper color. 'Strawberry Parfait' is scarlet;

Diascia barberae

Dimorphotheca sinuata

Dyssodia tenuiloba

. . . Dianthus

'Raspberry Parfait' is royal crimson. Magic Charms, an All-America Selection winner, produces abundant flowers (in five colors) on compact, vigorous plants. Both carnations and pinks have clumps of slim, pointed, silver-green leaves.

D. barbatus, sweet William, is usually grown as a biennial; but if started indoors in late winter, it will bloom the first year. It has broad, lance-shaped leaves of medium green. Its flowers are borne in clusters atop short stems. 'Wee Willie' blooms just 6 to 8 weeks from seed and grows 3 to 6 inches tall.

Culture. Chill seeds of *D. caryophyllus* for 1 to 2 weeks before sowing to improve germination. Leave seeds of *D. caryophyllus* uncovered; lightly cover seeds of *D. chinensis* and *D. barbatus*. Seeds germinate in 5 days at 70°F/21°C.

When seedlings are large enough to handle, transplant outdoors and grow at 50° to 55°F/10° to 13°C. Space plants 8 to 10 inches apart in well-drained soil. Pinch young plants to promote bushiness. For larger carnation flowers, remove all but one flower bud per plant.

DIASCIA BARBERAE
Twinspur
Scrophulariaceae

Flowers in: Summer
Colors: Rose-pink, deep pink, and coral
Exposure: Full sun; partial shade in hot-summer areas
Grows to: 12 inches
When to plant: Start seeds indoors 6 to 8 weeks before last frost or sow seeds outdoors after all danger of frost is past

This South African native is aptly named: the plant's flowers have two curving, hornlike spurs on the backs of the lower petals. Flowers are ¾ inch across and have yellow throats blotched with green. They appear in clusters at the ends of slender stems. The toothed leaves are small, glossy, and dark green. A fine choice for a rock garden, twinspur is easily propagated from cuttings. 'Pink Queen' produces 6-inch clusters of rose-pink flowers on 9- to 12-inch plants.

Culture. Seeds germinate in 15 days at 60°F/16°C. Twinspur flowers about 14 weeks after seeds are sown. Set plants out in spring in average soil, spacing them 6 inches apart. After the first flush of bloom, cut stalks back to the mound of foliage to encourage additional blossoms.

DIMORPHOTHECA
Cape marigold, African daisy
Compositae

Flowers in: Winter and early spring in mild-winter areas, summer in other climates
Colors: Shades of orange, red, pink, and white
Exposure: Full sun
Grows to: 12 inches
When to plant: Sow seeds outdoors in early spring in cold-winter climates, in fall in mild-winter areas

These valuable plants are free-blooming and provide broad masses of brilliant color during warm weather (they are not suited to cool coastal climates). *D. sinuata* (sold as *D. aurantiaca*) is perhaps the most familiar annual in this genus. The daisylike flowers come in a number of colors, most with contrasting dark centers. The spreading plants are useful as a ground cover, as an edging for a border, and as a filler among low-growing shrubs. The flowers are not useful for cut arrangements because they close at night and on cloudy days.

The hybrid 'Starshine' is a neat, mound-shaped, 12-inch-tall plant, covered with 2- to 3-inch-wide blooms in delicate shades of carmine, pink, rose, and white. Plants spread to 18 inches across. 'Tetra Goliath' has 3½-inch-wide flowers of vibrant orange on 12-inch plants. It thrives in summer heat.

D. pluvialis, the Cape marigold, has white flowers that are tinged with purple on the undersides of the petals. 'Glistening White' is a dwarf form, with flowers that are 4 inches across.

Culture. Seeds germinate in 7 to 14 days at 60° to 70°F/16° to 21°C. Plants are easy to grow in well-drained soil with full sun. Thin to 18 inches apart. Successive sowings will prolong the bloom season. *D. sinuata* reseeds itself in warm-winter areas.

DYSSODIA TENUILOBA
Dahlberg daisy, Golden fleece
Compositae

Flowers in: Summer to fall, extending to early winter in mild-winter climates
Colors: Yellow
Exposure: Full sun
Grows to: 12 inches
When to plant: Set out plants in spring after all danger of frost is past; in mild-winter climates, set out plants in fall or very early spring

With its sprawling habit and haze of fernlike foliage, the Dahlberg daisy is a perfect choice for hanging baskets and containers. It is also a good choice for edging a border or adding a spot of color in a rock garden. Finely divided, dark green foliage is clothed in golden yellow flowers up to ½ inch across. Native to Texas and Mexico, the plant grows well in hot-summer climates.

Culture. It is easiest to purchase plants from a nursery, as seeds can be difficult to start and plants can take 4 months to flower. Seeds germinate uncovered, in 10 to 16 days at 65° to 70°F/18° to 21°C. Plants grow best in sandy, well-drained soil. Space them 6 inches apart in the garden. Deadhead to promote flowering. Plants may live over in mild-winter climates, but they become straggly as they get older.

ESCHSCHOLZIA CALIFORNICA
California poppy
Papaveraceae

Flowers in: Early spring to summer
Colors: Shades of gold, orange, red, pink, and white
Exposure: Full sun
Grows to: 8 to 24 inches
When to plant: Sow seeds outdoors in fall or very early spring

This is the state flower of California, where it grows wild on hillsides and along roads. Its silky, brilliantly colored flowers dance above lacy foliage. It is easily grown and rewards even the most inexperienced gardener with myriads of satiny flowers that are up to 2 to 3 inches across. Foliage branches from the base of the plant and the leaves are finely cut and blue-green.

California poppy is wonderful for naturalizing, for covering sunny hillsides, or for planting in a dry rock garden. The flowers are short-lived when cut for arrangements; to use them at all, cut them while still furled. Grown in a border, California poppies must be deadheaded regularly or they will go to seed, with the foliage turning a straw color. Birds are attracted to the seed.

'Aurantiaca Orange King' grows 12 inches high and is early- and long-flowering, with intense orange single flowers. Thai Silk Mix offers uniform 10-inch plants with bronze-tinted foliage and 1½-inch semidouble fluted- and wavy-edged blooms in bright shades of red, pink, orange and gold. It is also available in a mixture of pink shades. 'Dalli' is a compact grower just 8 to 10 inches tall, and has stunning scarlet flowers with yellow throats and fluted petals.

Culture. Prepare the seedbed in fall. The plants do best in cool weather; early sowing, either in the fall or as soon as ground can be worked in very early spring, is advised. Seeds germinate in 7 to 14 days. Thin seedlings to 6 inches apart. The plants do not transplant well. In warm-winter climates, California poppies self-sow and come up year after year.

Eschscholzia californica

Euphorbia marginata

EUPHORBIA MARGINATA
Snow-on-the-mountain
Euphorbiaceae

Flowers in: Summer to fall
Colors: Foliage is a silvery green splashed with white
Exposure: Full sun to part shade
Grows to: 18 to 36 inches
When to plant: Sow seeds outdoors as soon as ground can be worked in spring

Grown for the attractive green-and-white coloration of the foliage, snow-on-the-mountain fills in attractively in the middle or back of a border. The oval, light green foliage is striped and margined with white on the upper leaves, with some of the topmost leaves nearly all white. The cool colors of the plant contrast well with brightly colored annuals. As the base of the plant is bare, it's a good idea to front it with shorter annuals. It provides complementary background for a mass of California poppies or dwarf zinnias. To use it in a flower bouquet, dip the cut ends of stems in boiling water or sear them over a flame; then arrange flowers in warm water in vases. 'Summer Icicle' is a dwarf variety, growing 18 inches tall with striking foliage. 'White Top' is uniform and erect, and grows to 36 inches tall.

Culture. Plant in average soil. Seeds germinate in 7 to 14 days. Thin plants to 12 inches apart. Transplant warily. Be careful when working with this plant, as its milky sap can irritate skin, eyes, and open cuts.

Felicia

Gaillardia

FELICIA
Blue daisy, Blue marguerite, Kingfisher daisy
Compositae

Flowers in: Spring to summer
Colors: Blue
Exposure: Full sun
Grows to: 18 inches
When to plant: Set out purchased plants in spring in cold-winter climates; plant in fall in mild-winter areas

Felicias are South African shrubby perennials, grown as annuals in cold-winter climates, with blue daisylike flowers. The low-growing plants have hairy leaves that are dark green, oval, and roughish. *F. amelloides*, the blue daisy or blue marguerite, has 1- to 3-inch-wide blossoms, blue with yellow centers, on plants growing to 18 inches tall. The plant will spread to 4 to 5 feet wide unless it is cut back. Keep it in shape by cutting often for flower arrangements (though flowers may close at night and on cloudy days). Its spreading habit makes it effective when planted at the top of a retaining wall or in a balcony planter from which it can cascade. 'George Lewis', 'Midnight', and 'Rhapsody in Blue' all have very dark blue flowers. 'Astrid Thomas' is dwarf, with medium blue flowers that remain open at night. There is also a white-flowered variety. 'San Luis', 'San Gabriel', and 'Santa Anita' have medium blue flowers that are 2½ to 3 inches across. The kingfisher daisy (*F. bergeriana*) grows just 6 inches tall and is a true annual. It flourishes in warm southern climates.

Culture. Purchased nursery-grown transplants can provide earlier bloom, as the plants require 3 to 4 months to bloom from seeds. Plant in well-drained soil. Provide water during dry weather. Pinch out the main shoot and side shoots when the plants are young to encourage compact growth. Shear plants back by a third when most of the flowers have gone to seed. They will quickly rebloom. Plant kingfisher daisies 6 to 12 inches apart in a sheltered, sunny spot.

GAILLARDIA PULCHELLA
Blanket flower
Compositae

Flowers in: Early summer to frost
Colors: Yellow, red, orange, and bicolors
Exposure: Full sun
Grows to: 24 inches
When to plant: Sow seeds outdoors after all danger of frost is past

Blanket flower provides sunny, vivid color in the garden and in cut arrangements. The warm-colored, sun-loving plants are especially appreciated when other flowers have been ruined by frost. Double and semidouble blooms rise on long, leafy stems above narrow, deeply cut, downy foliage. They are showy when massed together, and also are suitable for wildflower plantings. Since they grow well in dry soil, *gaillardias* are excellent choices for window boxes and containers. 'Red Plume', an All-America Selection, has a uniform dwarf habit and an extended

flowering season. The 12- to 14-inch plants are covered with brick red double blooms that are 1½ to 2 inches across, held well above the foliage. 'Yellow Sun' produces a dense mound of foliage with bright yellow, 2-inch, ball-shaped blooms and makes an excellent companion to red plume.

Culture. Sow seeds in well-drained soil. Seeds germinate in 14 to 21 days. Plants will not develop well in cold or heavy soils. Space 12 inches apart. Deadhead to encourage continued bloom.

GAZANIA RIGENS
Treasure flower
Compositae

Flowers in: Spring to early summer
Colors: Yellow, gold, cream, orange, pink, and bronzy red
Exposure: Full sun
Grows to: 12 inches
When to plant: Start seeds indoors 4 to 6 weeks before last frost; or purchase nursery-grown transplants to set out in spring after soil has warmed

These gaily colored perennials (grown as annuals in cold-winter climates) are best suited to desert gardens and are widely grown in the Southwest. The bright daisylike blossoms are up to 4 inches across, carried on stalks that rise 6 to 12 inches from the base of the plant. The shimmering petals surround dark centers, and the undersides of the petals are purplish. The 6- to 9-inch-long dark green leaves are sometimes lobed, are variable in shape,

Gazania rigens

and are felty on the undersides. Plants grow well in sites exposed to wind. The flowers close in overcast weather and at night, and so they are not good for cutting. Where the climate suits them, they make an attractive, free-blooming ground cover. They are dazzling when massed together. 'Moonglow' has bright yellow double blossoms that stay open even on dull days. The Chansonette Mixture has a good range of colors and is early-blooming and extra-compact. The 10-inch plants have 3-inch flowers in clear, bright colors. The Daybreak series is available in single colors of orange, yellow, bronze, and a mixture. 'Sunshine' has huge, 5-inch flowers with as many as 4 or 5 sharply defined blossom colors and silvery foliage on compact 6-inch plants. Carnival Mixed has mixed colors and gray-green foliage on 12-inch plants.

Culture. Gazania grows best where summer temperatures are in the 80°sF/27°C and 90°sF/32°C. It does not grow well where nights are cool or humidity is high. Space plants 8 to 12 inches apart in well-drained soil. Plants can be lifted in fall for colorful indoor display. If growing from seeds, cover the seeds lightly and then shade the flats to exclude all light. Maintain a temperature of 70°F/21°C. Seeds sown in mid-January should begin blooming in April.

GERBERA JAMESONII
Transvaal daisy
Compositae

Flowers in: Early summer and fall
Colors: Shades of pink, red, orange, yellow, and white
Exposure: Full sun; partial shade in hot-summer areas
Grows to: 8 to 18 inches
When to plant: Set out transplants in spring after soil has warmed

The Transvaal daisy is surely the most refined of the daisylike flowers. Its flower colors are deep, and all its forms—single, double, crested, and quilled—are elegant. It is grown as an annual in most climates, as a perennial in mild-winter climates. The plants spread slowly to form clumps of 9- to 10-inch-long lobed, medium green

leaves with woolly undersides. The flowers, with slender ray petals, rise above the foliage on erect or gracefully curving stems; they look handsome at the front of a border and make superior cut flowers. The Happipot strain is a dwarf, compact mixture 8 to 10 inches tall with red, rose, pink, salmon, orange, yellow, and cream blooms. The Skipper strain has smaller leaves and shorter flower stems and is suited to small container plantings or for use as an edging. The Tempo series offers dwarf plants in single shades of orange-scarlet, orange, rose-pink, scarlet, and yellow.

Culture. Transvaal daisies are somewhat difficult to grow from seed, and it is best to purchase transplants from the nursery. Plant in well-drained, fertile soil, being careful not to bury the crown. Space 12 to 15 inches apart. Protect from snails and slugs. Transvaal daisies prefer warm weather, but need afternoon shade and frequent watering where summers are hot and dry. However, plants will succumb quickly in poorly drained or soggy soils. If you are growing from seed, be sure to start with fresh seeds. Allow 4 to 6 weeks for germination at 70° to 75°F/21° to 24°C. When cutting flowers for arrangements, slit the bottom inch of the stem before placing in water.

Gerbera jamesonii

Gilia capitata

GILIA
Blue thimble flower, Bird's eyes
Polemoniaceae

Flowers in: Summer to early fall
Colors: Blue to violet
Exposure: Full sun
Grows to: 24 inches
When to plant: Sow seeds outdoors after all danger of frost is past

Gilia is a large genus comprising annuals, biennials, and perennials that are native to the American West and related to phlox. The annual forms are charming plants, covered with a profusion of small, showy flowers.

G. capitata, the blue thimble flower, is most widely available and withstands hot weather better than other species. Its tiny pale blue to violet blue flowers are held in dense, rounded clusters resembling pincushions. The finely cut foliage gives a lacy effect. While the flowers are small, they are so numerous that they make the whole plant beautiful. *G. tricolor,* bird's eyes, is a branching plant with finely cut leaves. Its pale- to deep-violet ½-inch flowers have yellow throats with purple spots; they are carried singly or in small clusters. Both species are good choices for a border, a rock garden, or a wildflower garden.

Culture. Plant in dry to average soil. Thin to 6 inches apart. Support taller varieties with brushy twigs. Plants are shallow-rooted, so provide water during extended dry periods. They grow best in cool-summer climates. Seeds germinate in 15 days at 68°F/20°C.

Gomphrena globosa

GOMPHRENA
Globe amaranth
Amaranthaceae

Flowers in: Summer to fall
Colors: Red, pink, white, orange, and purple
Exposure: Full sun
Grows to: 10 to 24 inches
When to plant: For earliest bloom, start seeds indoors 6 weeks before last frost; or sow outdoors, after all danger of frost is past

The cloverlike blossoms of globe amaranth are valued for fresh and dried bouquets, as well as for their handsome show in the garden. The mound-shaped plants are erect and well-branched, with oblong leaves of medium green. The small, dense flower heads are borne on long-stalked stems.

G. globosa has white, pink, lavender, red, or purple flowers. G. haageana has orange blossoms. The colors of globe amaranth are not especially harmonious and are best complemented by white flowers such as annual *Gypsophila* or white *Ageratum*.

Plants grow well in hot weather. The dwarf varieties make colorful edging plants, and taller varieties provide excellent cut flowers to use fresh or dried (they hold their color well when dried). 'Strawberry Fields' is the first true red *Gomphrena*, and 'Lavender Lady' blooms in a luscious lavender color. Both grow to 24 inches tall and produce a continuous bonanza of 1½-inch flowers. The Buddy series offers compact, 10- to 12-inch plants that bloom until frost; they are available in deep purple or white.

Culture. Soak seeds in water overnight before sowing. Seeds germinate in 10 to 14 days at 72°F/22°C. Plant in ordinary soil, thinning to 6 to 8 inches. Taller varieties benefit from staking. To dry blossoms, pick when blooms are thoroughly mature and hang them upside down in a shaded spot.

GYPSOPHILA ELEGANS
Annual baby's breath
Caryophyllaceae

Flowers in: Summer
Colors: White, pink, and red
Exposure: Full sun
Grows to: 18 inches
When to plant: Sow seeds outdoors in spring; for continuous bloom, sow again every 3 to 4 weeks from late spring into summer

Annual baby's breath has a multitude of dainty flowers that give the plant a misty, hazy effect. The single flowers are ½ inch or more across. The upright plant has lance-shaped leaves up to 3 inches long. Because the plants live for only 5 to 6 weeks, succession sowing is required to prolong the blooming season. This makes annual baby's breath somewhat of a chore to grow in a border. If you are willing to go to the trouble, try it as an airy blanket in front of gladiolus and other summer-blooming bulbs. It may be most suitable in a cutting garden; it makes an excellent addition to cut-flower arrangements. 'Covent Garden' has the largest white flowers. 'Kermesina' bears deep rose-colored blooms on plants that are 2½ feet tall.

Gypsophila elegans

Helianthus

Culture. Grow in average soil (rich soil will produce luxuriant growth that is easily beaten down in rainstorms). The genus name refers to the plant's preference for limestone (alkaline) soils. In areas where soils are strongly acidic, add lime before planting.

Scatter seed and tamp in firmly. Seeds germinate in about 10 days. Thin to 8 inches apart. Allow soil to dry between waterings. Early plantings may reseed themselves and bloom during the same season. When making successive sowings, harvest whole plants for indoor bouquets and replant with fresh seeds. To dry flowers for everlasting bouquets, hang upside down in a cool, dark place.

HELIANTHUS ANNUUS
Sunflower
Compositae

Flowers in: Summer
Colors: Creamy white, yellow, orange, maroon, and bicolors
Exposure: Full sun
Grows to: 24 inches to 12 feet
When to plant: Plant seeds outdoors after all danger of frost is past

Sunflowers are vigorous, erect, fast-growing plants with some of the largest flower heads any gardener could want to grow. The single and double flowers, which range from 4 to 24 inches across, are decorative no matter what their size. The plants are somewhat coarse, with rough, hairy stems and oval, coarsely serrated leaves. The central disk flowers are purplish brown, and are followed by edible seeds that are much-favored by birds. Tall sunflowers are effective in gardens with plants of similar height. They can be used as a hedge or fast-growing screen. The newer dwarf forms provide an impressive display when massed in large numbers.

'Sunbright' grows to 7 feet tall; its flowers have bright yellow, 4- to 6-inch petals. 'Giganteus' bears huge golden flowers that are 12 inches across on 10-foot plants. It is a good seed producer. Large-flowered Mix grows to 5 feet, with 6-inch flowers in yellow, red, and bronze, providing an impressive background of sparkling color. 'Luna' has 4- to 5-inch flowers in a delicate shade of yellow with rich chocolate centers. 'Italian White' has crisp, cream-colored, 4-inch flowers with a gold zone and black eye. 'Sunspot' is a breeding break through, with 10-inch yellow flowers on 24-inch-tall plants. It yields a bounty of seeds.

Culture. Plant in average soil. Seeds germinate in 10 days. Thin to 18 inches apart. Tall varieties should be staked, as the flower heads become heavy when seeds are formed. To save seeds for winter bird food, remove heads as soon as the seeds have matured. Otherwise, the birds will help themselves.

HELICHRYSUM BRACTEATUM
Strawflower
Compositae

Flowers in: Summer
Colors: Yellow, orange, red, pink, and white
Exposure: Full sun
Grows to: 12 to 36 inches
When to plant: Plant seeds outdoors in spring in areas with long growing seasons; in areas with shorter growing seasons, start seeds indoors 4 to 6 weeks before last frost

The papery flowers of strawflower hold their color indefinitely when dried. They are also beautiful in fresh arrangements. The tiny flowers in the center of the blossom are surrounded by stiff, colored leaves called bracts. Straplike, medium green leaves are 2 to 5 inches long. The taller varieties can offer a colorful accent, but they become leggy, require staking, and are

Helichrysum bracteatum

best planted at the back of a garden. Dwarf varieties provide bright color for rock gardens. The Bikini series has compact 12-inch-tall plants covered with brilliant 2-inch flowers; it is available in pink, gold, white, and a bright red. Bright Bikinis Mixture has a blend of dark red, bright yellow, red, hot pink, and white. Pastel Mix offers 2-inch flowers in soft tones that blend well with other flower colors. *H. subulifolium* 'Golden Star' has dainty, 1½-inch, lemon yellow flowers on mounded 15-inch-tall plants.

Culture. Strawflowers thrive in dry areas and on hillsides. Sow seeds in well-drained, average soil. Seeds should germinate in 7 to 10 days at 70° to 75°F/21° to 24°C. Thin to 12 inches apart. To dry, pick flowers that are fully open; hang them upside down in a shady spot.

HELIOTROPIUM ARBORESCENS
Heliotrope, Cherry pie
Boraginaceae

Flowers in: Summer
Colors: Purple, white, and deep blue
Exposure: Full sun
Grows to: 8 to 24 inches
When to plant: Set out transplants in spring after soil has warmed

Once experienced, the rich, romantic scent of old-fashioned heliotrope is never forgotten. The fragrance is sweet and vanillalike, without being cloying. The handsome, branching plants have dark green, rough-textured foli-

Heliotropium arborescens

age that complements lighter-colored foliage. Leaves are lance-shaped and deeply veined. The flowers grow in large, dense clusters. The plants are perennial in their native Peru and other mild-winter areas, but are grown as annuals in much of cold-winter North America.

Heliotrope makes a decorative display in borders as well as in cut-flower arrangements. It is set off to advantage by companion plantings of lighter colored flowers such as sweet alyssum or marigolds. Massed plantings provide more perfume. If you grow heliotrope in containers, you can place the pots where its fragrance can be best enjoyed.

'Mini Marine' is very fragrant; deep purple flower clusters that are 8 to 12 inches across provide a rich display in early summer. The compact, bushy plant grows 8 to 10 inches tall, and is good as a winter house plant. 'Marine' grows to 18 inches, with royal purple flowers. 'Black Beauty' and 'Iowa' bear deep purple flowers.

Culture. Purchase nursery-grown transplants to set out in spring, spacing them 12 inches apart. Plant in rich, fertile soil. Place containers with heliotrope in spots with afternoon shade. Avoid overwatering, as the fragrance is intensified when growing conditions are on the dry side. Cuttings root easily in water or moist loam. Plants may be lifted and brought indoors, but require cool, moist growing conditions. Seeds germinate in 7 to 21 days at 70° to 80°F/21° to 27°C, and must be started 10 to 12 weeks before setting out.

Helipterum roseum

HELIPTERUM ROSEUM (ACROCLINIUM ROSEUM)
Strawflower
Compositae

Flowers in: Summer
Colors: Yellow, pink, rose, carmine, and white
Exposure: Full sun
Grows to: 12 to 24 inches
When to plant: Plant seeds outdoors in spring after the danger of frost is past

Helipterum is another easily grown annual everlasting that is commonly called strawflower (see also *Helichrysum*). A wildflower in Australia, it has double daisylike flowers. The narrow, pointed, medium green leaves are numerous toward the tops of the stems. Flowers hold their color for long periods. The ray petals are thicker, with a brownish or greenish tinge toward the

Iberis

base. Use flowers dried, in winter arrangements.

H. roseum grandiflorum has harmonious hues of rose, carmine, and white on distinctly larger flowers.

Culture. Plant in average soil. Thin seedlings to 9 inches apart. To dry flowers, cut when the blossoms are fully open and hang them upside down in a shady spot.

IBERIS
Candytuft
Cruciferae

Flowers in: Spring and summer
Colors: White, pink, red, purple, and lavender
Exposure: Full sun, partial shade in hot summer areas
Grows to: 12 to 24 inches
When to plant: Sow seeds outdoors in early spring; in mild-winter climates, sow in fall for early-spring flowering

The flowers of candytuft cluster in showy spikes or globes. Rocket candytuft (*I. amara coronaria*) has fragrant white blossoms up to 1 inch across in dense hyacinthlike clusters on stems that grow 12 to 24 inches tall. It is dramatic in a border or in cut flower arrangements.

Globe candytuft (*I. umbellata*) has tiny flowers in flattened cones; it grows 7 to 12 inches tall. Sometimes confused with sweet alyssum, globe candytuft is also a useful edging plant and is a good-looking addition to a rock garden. In addition to white, globe candytuft is available in intense shades of red and purple.

Both candytufts have dark green leaves that are narrow and lance-shaped. Both are most floriferous where summer nights are cool. 'Mount Hood' rocket candytuft produces fragrant, pure white blooms on 24-inch stems. The Flash series (*I. umbellata*) grows up to 10 inches tall, in a bright blend of rosy colors.

Culture. Plant in average soil. Seeds germinate in 7 to 14 days. Thin to 6 to 9 inches apart. In hot-summer areas, plant in light shade and provide plenty of water during periods of heat and drought.

Impatiens

IMPATIENS
Garden balsam, Busy Lizzy
Balsaminaceae

Flowers in: Early summer to fall
Colors: White; shades of red, pink, orange, lavender; and bicolors
Exposure: Full sun to shade, depending on species
Grows to: 8 to 30 inches, depending on species
When to plant: Set out transplants in spring when all danger of frost is past

Impatiens includes annuals and, in some areas, tender perennials grown as annuals. The name refers to the tendency of the seed pod, when barely touched, to split open and "impatiently" shoot out its seeds.

Impatiens wallerana, the most widely grown kind of *impatiens*, is invaluable in shady gardens. The plants provide mounds of bright color throughout the season. The flowers, borne on short stems, are 1 to 2 inches wide, single and double, in vivid as well as pastel hues. The dark green coloring of the broad, pointed leaves is a perfect foil for the blossoms. *Impatiens* are excellent accent plants among shade-loving perennials such as hosta and ferns, and are useful in small beds ringing the trunks of mature shade trees. Planted in single or mixed colors, they make beautiful edgings for shaded borders. Their base-branching habit quickly produces a carpet of color. They are tender perennials, grown as annuals in cold-winter climates, and will reseed themselves in mild-winter areas. The Dazzler series is compact, growing 8 to 10 inches tall, in a dozen luminous, fade-resistant colors. The Super Elfin strain has large blooms in 16 colors on uniform, compact plants. The Shady Lady series includes some excellent garden performers. The Blitz series has the largest flowers, available in 7 colors, and is suited for hanging baskets. In the Showstopper series, noted for its large blooms, 'Showstopper Pink and White' is a charming bicolor, and 'Showstopper Flair' offers a spectacular display of pale pink blooms with hot pink centers. This series is also good for hanging baskets. Accent has strong, early-blooming plants with 2-inch flowers in 15 single colors and 5 bicolors called Accent Star. 'Mega' bears large flowers displaying bright orange-and-white stars. Among the double impatiens, the Duet series has full blossoms combining white with red, orange, scarlet, or deep rose. The compact Rosebud series is good for hanging baskets and containers, and comes in 7 colors. This series must be propagated from cuttings, and is not available in seed form.

New Guinea hybrid impatiens have handsome bronze, green, or variegated leaves, striped with cream or red, and extra-large single flowers. This species generally requires more sun than the common impatiens. These plants are also tender perennials grown as annuals and are good choices for containers. The Spectra strain combines bronze, green, and variegated foliage with large blooms of white, pink, carmine, rose, light lavender, deep orchid, coral, red, and scarlet on 10- to 14-inch plants. 'Tango', an All-America Selection, grows to 24 inches tall, with large single flowers in a glowing orange color.

Balsam (I. balsamina) grows 24 to 30 inches tall with 1- to 2-inch-wide mostly double flowers. It grows well in sun where summers are cool or in shade in hot-summer areas. Bush-type balsams display their flowers near the tops of the plants. Otherwise, flowers are somewhat hidden, as they are borne amid foliage along the tall, erect main stem. The bright green leaves of this old-fashioned true annual are up to 6 inches long and are pointed and deeply serrated. The flowers do not last long when cut. The Color Parade mix has pastel blooms in orange, rose, white, and pink on 14- to 16-inch plants. This is the type with blooms hidden within the foliage, and is best used for bedding. The double flowers of the dwarf Carambole strain are held well above the foliage. The plants grow to 14 inches tall.

Culture. All the species require plenty of moisture, especially during the heat of summer. *I. wallerana* and New Guinea hybrids are somewhat difficult to grow from seed, and it is best to purchase transplants from a nursery. Space plants 9 to 12 inches apart. *I. wallerana* will grow taller when set close together. If you grow these from seeds, expect germination in 10 to 20 days at 75° to 78°F/24° to 26°C. Light, uniform soil temperature, and moisture are very important when growing *I. wallerana* from seed. Balsam can be started indoors 4 to 6 weeks before last frost, then planted out after all danger of frost is past. Seeds germinate in 8 to 10 days. All species transplant well.

IPOMOEA TRICOLOR
Morning glory
Convolvulaceae

Flowers in: Summer to frost
Colors: Blue, white, pink, red, chocolate, crimson, lavender, and violet
Exposure: Full sun
Grows to: Climber, to 10 feet; dwarf forms to 5 inches
When to plant: Sow seeds outdoors after all danger of frost is past

For fast-growing vining cover and showy blossoms, morning glory is unsurpassed. Its large flowers (3 to 5 inches wide) display rich colors of purple, pink, or blue with a paler tube, sometimes striped or margined with a contrasting color. Flowers of older varieties open only from dawn to midmorning, but newer varieties stay open most of the day. The plants have large heart-shaped, 4- to 5-inch-long leaves and vining tendrils. Morning glory is eye-stopping grown on trellises, fences, or arbors. 'Heavenly Blue' has intense blue color that lightens toward the center. 'Pearly Gates' has enormous white flowers. The Early Call mix has

Ipomoea tricolor

white, pink, crimson, lavender-pink, light blue, and violet flowers. Dwarf variegated strains have variegated leaves and blooms, with rosy red, pink, chocolate, and sky blue flowers, all with white margins. The plants grow to 5 inches high and 8 inches across.

Ipomoea alba, moonflower, is a climbing plant, up to 10 to 20 feet, that has magnificent, sweet-scented, large white flowers. The blossoms, up to 6 inches across, open in the early evening and close the next morning. Use moonflowers for quick screening on an arbor, trellis, or fence. They can become a nuisance, as they often self-sow.

Ipomoea nil (*I. imperialis*) includes the large-flowered Imperial Japanese strains. 'Chocolate' has huge saucer-shaped flowers in a soft chocolate-pink color. 'Scarlett O'Hara' has rosy red flowers.

Cypress vine (*I. quamoclit*) has narrow, threadlike foliage and small, 1½-inch-long scarlet flowers. Hybrid 'Cardinal Climber' has deeply lobed leaves and a profusion of small, 1- to 2-inch-long red flowers that often attract hummingbirds.

Culture. The seeds are very hard; for good germination, nick seed coats with a file or soak in lukewarm water overnight. Plant ½ inch deep in average soil, 8 to 12 inches apart. Seeds germinate in 7 to 21 days. For earliest blooms, plants may be started indoors, at 70° to 75°F/21° to 24°C, in peat pots. Overwatering and overfertilization encourage excess foliage at the expense of flowers. Morning glories reseed themselves, but these volunteers usually are inferior in bloom color and size.

Kochia scoparia

KOCHIA SCOPARIA
Summer cypress, Burning bush
Chenopodiaceae

Flowers in: Grown for foliage only
Colors: Light green during summer, bright red in fall
Exposure: Full sun
Grows to: 36 inches
When to plant: Start seeds indoors 6 to 8 weeks before last frost

Summer cypress has a dense form and soft, feathery foliage in a pleasing shade of green. It can be sheared to any desired shape or height. It can be used as a formal accent in a border and makes a fine low-growing temporary hedge. It grows well in hot-summer areas, and its erect habit suits it to windy locations. The plant is a good choice for containers mixed with low-growing or trailing plants. Flowers are insignificant. The foliage can be used to good effect in cut flower arrangements. *K. s. trichophylla,* burning bush, has the same growth habit, but its foliage turns scarlet to maroon at the first frost.

Culture. Soak seeds for 24 hours before sowing. Seeds germinate, uncovered, in 10 to 15 days at 50°F/10°C. Set out transplants after all danger of frost is past. Plant in average, well-drained soil, 2 feet apart (or 8 inches apart for a hedge). Growth is slow early in the season and increases with the onset of warm weather. In mild-winter climates, plants reseed themselves and the profusion of volunteers can become a nuisance.

LATHYRUS ODORATUS
Sweet pea
Leguminosae

Flowers in: Spring, continuing into summer in cool-summer climates
Colors: Shades of pink, red, purple, lavender, white, cream, apricot, salmon, maroon, and bicolors
Exposure: Full sun
Grows to: Climbers to 5 feet; bush-type 12 to 36 inches
When to plant: Sow seeds outdoors as soon as soil can be worked in early spring. In mild-winter climates, sow in fall for early-spring bloom. Early-flowering types can be sown in mild-winter climates in late summer or early fall for winter bloom

The lovely, fragrant sweet pea is the quintessential flowering plant in British gardens. In the United States, sweet peas are best grown in similar cool, moist climates, such as the Pacific Northwest and coastal New England. But with proper care and selection of early-blooming cultivars, sweet peas can also be enjoyed, even if briefly, in warm climates.

The sweet pea flower is made up of a large rounded petal (called the banner or standard), two narrow side petals (wings), and two lower petals that are somewhat united (keel). They are held in clusters on long stems, making them excellent for cut flower arrangements. The old varieties were known for their sweet fragrance. Many newer ones have little or no fragrance. Oval leaves, somewhat pointed, are light green to blue-green. The bush types make pretty mounds of color, and soften the front part of a border. In hot-summer areas, plan on replanting spots sweet peas have occupied with warm-weather annuals.

The Early Mammoth strain is an early-blooming climber with exceptionally large and wavy-edged blossoms in a rich mix of colors. The Con-

Lathyrus odoratus

Lavatera trimestris

tinental strain is a well-balanced, very early-blooming mix of shades of red, salmon, blue, lavender, and white. Its erect habit makes plants, which grow to 24 to 30 inches tall, require a minimum of support. 'Little Sweetheart', growing to just 12 inches tall, was bred especially for containers and hanging baskets. It presents a colorful display of red, pink, rose, white, purple, lilac, and blue flowers. The Bijou Mixed strain grows to 15 inches tall and is heat resistant.

Culture. Sweet peas require rich, deeply dug soil. It is best to prepare the soil in fall, digging a trench 24 inches deep, adding a 4-inch layer of compost or manure, and filling with topsoil to make a mounded seedbed. The mounding will improve drainage and permit earlier planting in spring.

Early sowing is important, as sweet peas grow best in cool, moist weather. Immerse seeds in warm water and soak them for 24 hours before sowing. Plant as soon as the soil is workable. Sow 6 inches apart in single rows, or 12 inches apart in double rows; treat the rows with a legume innoculant. Seeds germinate in 14 to 21 days.

Prepare trellis or string supports for climbing types as soon as seeds have been planted (or plant in front of a wire fence). Small brushy twigs can be placed in the rows for early training. Allow for good air circulation all around the support.

Be sure to cut off all seed pods: once a plant starts to set seed, it will cease blooming. To keep your sweet peas in bloom, cut flowers when buds break and use them in indoor bouquets. Provide plenty of water during the growing season, and mulch plants early to preserve moisture and keep roots cool.

Limonium sinuatum

LAVATERA TRIMESTRIS
Tree mallow
Malvaceae

Flowers in: Summer to early fall
Colors: White, pink, and red
Exposure: Full sun
Grows to: 36 inches to 6 feet
When to plant: Sow seeds outdoors in early spring

The satiny hibiscuslike flowers of tree mallow can light up the middle or back of a cool-summer border. Single flowers are up to 3 inches across. The foliage, shaped like maple leaves, is medium to dark green. It can also be used as a fast-growing summer hedge. 'Mont Rose' has rose-pink flowers; 'Mont Blanc' has white flowers. Both grow to 21 inches tall. 'Silver Cup' has 4-inch, chalice-like pink flowers.

Culture. Plants grow best in moist, cool-summer climates. Plant in average soil, spaced 24 inches apart. Seeds germinate in 14 to 21 days. To extend the bloom season, make several successive sowings. Stake tall varieties.

Linaria maroccana

LIMONIUM SINUATUM
Statice
Plumbaginaceae

Flowers in: Summer
Colors: Blue, lavender, white, rose, yellow, apricot, and peach
Exposure: Full sun
Grows to: 10 to 48 inches
When to plant: Sow seeds outdoors in early spring or start indoors 8 to 10 weeks before the last frost

Delicate statice is decorative in fresh and dried bouquets. The small, ⅜-inch papery flowers are borne in flat-topped clusters on many-branched, winged stems. The deeply lobed, lance-shaped leaves form a rosette at the base of the plant. This Mediterranean native is a good choice for Pacific Coast gardens. The Soirée strain blooms early, with richly colored flowers on 24- to 30-inch stems. The Dwarf Biedermeier strain has vivid blooms and grows just 10 to 12 inches tall, making it useful for bedding as well as cutting. Petite Bouquet has compact 12-inch plants in a range of colors.

L. suworowii, Russian statice, has well-branched, curved spikes of bright rose or lilac flowers. The rose-colored variety grows to 18 inches, while the lilac variety is extra-tall, reaching 3½ to 4 feet.

Culture. Plant in average, well-drained soil. Water deeply but infrequently. Seeds germinate in 14 to 21 days at 75° to 80°F/24° to 27°C. Thin to 9 to 12 inches apart. Continued cutting of the flowers encourages prolonged bloom.

LINARIA MAROCCANA
Toadflax
Scrophulariaceae

Flowers in: Early summer to fall; winter- to spring-blooming in mild-winter climates
Colors: Red, rose, pink, lavender, blue, purple, gold, yellow, cream, and bicolors
Exposure: Full sun or light shade
Grows to: 12 to 24 inches
When to plant: Sow seeds outdoors as soon as ground can be worked; in mild-winter areas, sow in fall for winter-spring bloom

Linum grandiflorum

A member of the snapdragon family, toadflax has dainty, brightly colored blossoms on slender spikes. The ½-inch blossoms often have contrasting throats. The medium green foliage is very narrow. Toadflax can provide jewel-like color at the front of a border. The Fairy Lights strain grows to 12 inches and has contrasting white throats. The Northern Lights mixture has bright colors on 24-inch-tall plants.

Culture. Easily grown. Sow in ordinary soil. Seeds germinate in 7 to 14 days. Thin to 6 inches apart.

LINUM GRANDIFLORUM
Flowering flax
Linaceae

Flowers in: Spring into summer
Colors: Red, white, and pink
Exposure: Full sun
Grows to: 12 to 30 inches
When to plant: Sow seeds outdoors as soon as ground can be worked in spring; in mild-winter areas, sow in fall for spring bloom

The glowing flowers of annual flax are delightful in mixed beds and borders. The 1- to 2-inch-wide blooms have five petals and last only a single day. The gray-green leaves are slender and grasslike. 'Bright Eyes' provides bushy, 30-inch-tall plants bearing pure white blooms that are 2 inches across, with bright crimson centers. 'Rubrum' has brilliant blood-red flowers with a satiny sheen on 15- to 18-inch plants.

(Continued on next page)

Lobelia erinus

. . . *Linum grandiflorum*

Culture. Flax is easy to grow but difficult to transplant. Plant in ordinary soil. Sow thickly. Seeds can take 3 to 4 weeks to germinate. Thin to 8 to 12 inches apart. Successive sowings will prolong the bloom season. Plants often reseed themselves, without becoming a nuisance.

LOBELIA ERINUS
Lobeliaceae

Flowers in: Summer to frost
Colors: Blue, white, red, and pink
Exposure: Full sun; partial shade in hot-summer climates
Grows to: 4 to 6 inches
When to plant: Set out transplants in spring after all danger of frost is past

Lobelia can be a very successful choice for hanging baskets and window boxes, from which its richly colored flowers can cascade. Its compact, spreading habit makes it useful for edging and in rock gardens. The dainty, lipped blossoms often have contrasting white or yellowish throats. Small, narrow, green or bronze leaves grow thickly on well-branched stems.

Lobelia blooms best where summer nights are cool. Early-blooming 'Blue Moon' is more heat tolerant than other varieties, and has ½-inch-wide, violet-blue flowers on upright, 5-inch-tall plants. The Fountain series has a lush, cascading habit with light blue, lilac, rose, and white flowers. 'Sapphire' has blue flowers with white eyes on a cascading plant. 'Rosamunde' has carmine-red blooms with white eyes on bronze-foliaged dwarf plants. 'Crystal Palace' has bronze-green foliage with dark blue flowers on 4- to 6-inch plants. 'White Lady' produces snow-white blooms.

Culture. *Lobelia* grows slowly and can take 2 months from seed to planting-out size. It is easiest to start with transplants from a nursery. Plant *lobelia* in ordinary soil, spacing plants 6 inches apart. Pinch to promote bushiness. After first blooms begin to fade, cut back by half to prolong flowering. *Lobelia* sometimes lives over in mild-winter climates. Provide plenty of water during dry periods. Seeds germinate, uncovered, in 20 days at 70° to 75°F/ 21° to 24°C.

LOBULARIA MARITIMA
Sweet alyssum
Cruciferae

Flowers in: Spring to hard frost; all year in mild-winter climates
Colors: White, cream, rose, pink, purple, violet, and lavender
Exposure: Full sun to light shade
Grows to: 4 to 6 inches
When to plant: Sow seeds outdoors in spring. For winter bloom, sow in fall in mild-winter areas

The honey-scented flowers of sweet alyssum literally cover the plant throughout the season. Sweet alyssum is one of the best annuals for edging the front of a bed or border. Its low-growing habit makes it a good choice for rock gardens and for planting between flagstones or pavers. It is attractive when planted at the top of a retaining wall or in hanging baskets, where its trailing habit can be used to advantage. It grows rapidly and flowers quickly from seeds; it can be started almost any time during the growing season. Its small green leaves are completely hidden by clusters of tiny, four-petaled blossoms.

'Carpet of Snow' has pure white flowers on 3- to 4-inch plants. 'Oriental Night' has dark violet blooms on spreading plants up to 8 inches across.

Lobularia maritima

Lychnis coeli-rosa

'Rosie O'Day' has lavender-rose flowers on plants that spread up to 10 inches across. Easter Bonnet and Pastel Carpet strains are beautiful mixtures, the former in shades of purple, rose, lavender and white, the latter a blend of cream, lilac, pink, rose, violet, and white.

Culture. Plant in average soil. Seeds germinate in 8 to 10 days. Thin to 6 to 8 inches apart. (If you are starting seeds indoors, sow seeds, uncovered, in sixpacks since small seedlings are difficult to transplant.) If flowering diminishes, cut plants back by half and fertilize to encourage additional blossoms. Plants sometimes reseed themselves. In mild-winter climates, they will bloom year-round.

LYCHNIS COELI-ROSA
Rose-of-heaven
Caryophyllaceae

Flowers in: Summer; winter to spring in mild-winter climates
Colors: Blue, lavender, white, and pink
Exposure: Full sun
Grows to: 9 to 18 inches
When to plant: Sow seeds outdoors in early spring; in mild-winter areas, sow in fall

Rose-of-heaven is a graceful plant, with upward-facing, saucer-shaped flowers. The single flowers, up to 1 inch across, generally have a contrasting lighter or darker eye. The green or blue-green leaves are long, narrow, and sharply pointed. The plant is good for cutting and bedding and is charming in a container.

Culture. Plant in average soil. Thin to 4 inches apart. Plants bloom early.

Matthiola incana

MATTHIOLA
Stock
Cruciferae

Flowers in: Spring into summer
Colors: White, cream, apricot, lavender, purple, shades of pink and red, and bicolors
Exposure: Full sun
Grows to: 12 to 30 inches
When to plant: Sow seeds outdoors in early spring; in mild-winter climates, sow in fall for late-winter and early-spring bloom

Few flowers offer the unique fragrance of stocks. Planted next to walkways or windows, their intense, spicy aroma fills the air with heady echoes of cinnamon and clove. The single or double flowers cluster thickly along sturdy flower spikes, and are a reliable backbone for cut-flower arrangements. Foliage is gray-green and lance-shaped. *Matthiola* thrives in cool weather; some newer varieties tolerate heat.

Matthiola incana is the most common species. The Giant Imperials series is widely available in a mixture of colors and grows 18 to 24 inches tall. The Midget series offers uniform, compact, 8- to 10-inch plants with well-formed, fully double flower spikes in vibrant colors, available in single or mixed colors. The Midget series is heat tolerant, although it does best in cool temperatures. The Trisomic Seven-Week series performs well because its double-flowered plants don't set seeds. Dwarf Stockpot can be in full flower 7 to 9 weeks from sowing. 'Beauty of Nice' blooms over a longer period than the early varieties. *Matthiola longipetala bicornis* (night-scented stock) has lilac flowers on 12 to 18 inch stems and a pronounced scent that's most powerful in the evening.

Culture. Choose moderately rich, moist soil in full sun. Sow seeds outdoors as soon as soil can be worked, or start seeds indoors 6 to 8 weeks before average date of last frost. Seeds germinate in 14 to 18 days at 65° to 75°F/18° to 24°C. In beds and borders, space plants 9 to 12 inches apart. Water regularly throughout the growing and flowering period.

MIMULUS HYBRIDUS
Monkey flower
Scrophulariaceae

Flowers in: Summer
Colors: Shades of red, yellow, and orange
Exposure: Partial to full shade
Grows to: 12 to 18 inches
When to plant: Sow seeds outdoors in spring, or set out transplants in spring

The showy, velvety blossoms of monkey flower appear on low-growing, mound-shaped plants. The two-lipped flowers, up to 2 inches across, come in bright colors that are often spotted, and give the impression of a smiling monkey face. Succulent, serrated leaves are light to medium green. Monkey flower can provide warm, bright color at the front of a shady border, and its spreading habit makes it fill out hanging baskets and containers quickly. It grows best in cool, moist climates and is prized in the Pacific Northwest. The Calypso strain has 16- to 18-inch-tall plants with solid and bicolor blooms of gold, wine, and fire-red. The Mystic strain has solid-colored blooms in orange, rose, and yellow on compact, spreading plants. It can tolerate heat better than the other varieties.

Culture. Sow or plant in moist, humus-rich soil. Seeds germinate in 5 to

Mimulus

Mirabilis jalapa

7 days at 60° to 70°F/16° to 21°C. Space 6 inches apart. Plants require plenty of water. Cut back after the first flush of flowers to promote bushiness and continued bloom. Cuttings root easily in sand.

MIRABILIS JALAPA
Four o'clock, Marvel of Peru
Nyctaginaceae

Flowers in: Summer to fall
Colors: Shades of yellow, red, white, and pink
Exposure: Full sun
Grows to: 24 inches to 4 feet
When to plant: Sow seeds outdoors in spring

These old-fashioned plants are called four o'clocks for their flowers' habit of opening in late afternoon. The fragrant, 2-inch-long, trumpet-shaped blossoms, often mottled or striped, close again in morning, but stay open all day on cloudy days. Plants bloom profusely throughout summer. The dark green, 2- to 6-inch-long leaves are borne on erect, well-branched stems. Try this plant in the middle of a border or grow it in containers. The blossoms attract hummingbirds.

Note: All parts of the plant are poisonous.

Culture. Sow in average soil, thinning to 12 to 24 inches apart. Seeds germinate in 10 to 14 days. The plant often reseeds itself and is considered perennial in mild-winter climates. Its tuberous roots can be dug in fall and stored over the winter like dahlia roots.

Moluccella laevis

Myosotis sylvatica

Nemesia strumosa

MOLUCCELLA LAEVIS
Bells-of-Ireland
Labiatae

Flowers in: Summer
Colors: White or pale pink blossoms set in pale green cups
Exposure: Full sun
Grows to: 15 to 36 inches
When to plant: Sow seeds outdoors in early spring; in mild-winter climates, sow seed outdoors in late fall

The unusual spikes of bells-of-Ireland make an interesting addition to a mixed border. Each erect stem bears clusters of tiny fragrant flowers, set inside enlarged calyxes (the outer leaves that appear at the base of most flowers). The calyxes are ornamented with a network of delicate white veins. Leaves of this Mediterranean native are rounded and coarsely toothed. The flowers are charming in bouquets, and can also be dried for use in winter arrangements.

Culture. Sow in loose, well-drained soil while the ground is still cool. Germination is best at about 50°F/10°C and can take 3 to 5 weeks. Thin to 12 inches apart. Seedlings are difficult to transplant. To dry the flowers, pick off the leaves along a stem and hang the stems upside down in a cool, dark, well-ventilated spot. The flowers are wheat-colored when dried.

MYOSOTIS SYLVATICA
Forget-me-not
Boraginaceae

Flowers in: Spring; winter in mild-winter areas
Colors: Blue; also pink and white
Exposure: Light shade
Grows to: 6 to 12 inches
When to plant: Sow seeds outdoors in fall; in cold-winter climates, sow indoors in winter and set out transplants in early spring

Forget-me-not is widely planted in English gardens. The plant's loose sprays of fragrant, pastel flowers make a fine springtime sight when interplanted with tulips. It prefers cool, moist growing conditions, and is best grown in woodland gardens, around the edges of ponds, or along the banks of a stream. Leaves are dark green, narrow, and lance-shaped. The flowers are long-lasting when cut. 'Victoria Blue' forms mound-shaped plants, 6 to 8 inches high, with gentian-blue flowers.

Culture. Plant in moist, fertile soil. Seeds germinate in 8 to 14 days at 68°F/20°C. Thin to 6 to 8 inches apart. Forget-me-not grows best where the spring season is long and cool. Plants die back in the heat of summer, but may reseed and come up in late summer, providing beautiful fall color.

NEMESIA STRUMOSA
Scrophulariaceae

Flowers in: Winter to spring in mild-winter climates; summer elsewhere
Colors: White, yellow, red, pink, lavender, blue, and bicolors
Exposure: Full sun
Grows to: 8 to 18 inches
When to plant: Sow seeds outdoors in fall in mild-winter areas, in spring in cold-winter climates

This South African native thrives in cool-summer climates where nighttime temperatures drop below 65°F/18°C. Its small, cup-shaped, ¾-inch-diameter flowers are carried in clusters 3 to 4 inches deep. The flowers have an enlarged lower lip and resemble snapdragons and *linarias*, plants that are related to them. The jewel-toned blossoms are borne above lance-shaped, serrated leaves. A handsome edging plant, *nemesia* is also good for growing in containers. It is a colorful addition to a rock garden.

'National Ensign' has bright red and pure white bicolored blooms on bushy, compact, 8-inch plants. The Tapestry strain has a rich mix of colors on upright, 10-inch plants. Carnival has brilliant flowers on compact plants.

Culture. Sow in rich, moist, well-drained soil. Germination takes 7 to 14 days at temperatures between 60° and 68°F/16° and 20°C. (For early bloom, start seeds indoors.) Thin to 6 inches apart. Pinch to promote bushy growth, and cut back by half after the first flush of bloom. *Nemesia* blooms best in cool weather.

Nemophila menziesii

NEMOPHILA
Baby blue eyes, Five spot
Hydrophyllaceae

Flowers in: Spring
Colors: Blue and white
Exposure: Full sun to partial shade
Grows to: 10 to 12 inches
When to plant: Sow seeds outdoors in early spring; in mild-winter climates, sow outdoors in fall

Baby blue eyes (also called California bluebell) and five spot are dainty, clean-looking California wildflowers. They thrive in the cool Western coastal and mountain climates. Both are trailing plants, growing to 12 inches long, with bell-shaped, single flowers up to 1 inch across. Pale green, hairy, fern-like foliage gives the plants a delicate appearance. Baby blue eyes (*N. menziesii*) has bright blue flowers with pale centers. Five spot (*N. maculata*) has white flowers with a prominent bluish-purple spot at the edge of each of the five petals. The plants form an attractive ground cover among spring-blooming bulbs.

Culture. Plant in moist soil, and supply constant moisture. Seeds germinate in 7 to 12 days. Thin to 6 inches apart. *Nemophila* dislikes transplanting and is quickly killed by heat and humidity. Plants reseed themselves in favorable sites.

Nicotiana alata

NICOTIANA
Flowering tobacco
Solanaceae

Flowers in: Spring through summer
Colors: White, pink, red, purple, and green
Exposure: Full sun to light shade
Grows to: 10 inches to 4 feet
When to plant: Sow seeds indoors 6 to 8 weeks before last frost; set out transplants in spring after all danger of frost is past

Flowering tobacco is an old-fashioned annual grown for its stately elegance and evening fragrance. Newer varieties offer compact plants with rosy flowers that bloom all season and open during the day. Relatives of smoking tobacco, *N. alata* and *N. sylvestris* are tender perennials from South America, grown as annuals in this country; in warm-winter areas they may live over. *N. alata* has soft, sticky, oval leaves that are 2 to 3 inches long. Its tubular flowers, 2 to 3 inches long and 1 to 2 inches across, are borne in clusters on erect stems. For strong, sweet fragrance, especially at night, plant *N. alata* 'Grandiflora', which grows 24 to 36 inches tall, with pure white, night-blooming flowers. Newer varieties of *N. alata* are more dwarf and, generally, not fragrant. The Nicki series is a vigorous grower, to 24 inches, and includes a beautiful red variety. The Domino series is compact, growing 10 to 14 inches tall. It blooms well during summer heat, with flowers in pink, purple, red, green, and white. The Starship series is excellent for mass plantings. It is more compact, with flowers in lemon-lime, red, rose-pink, and white. *N. sylvestris* grows to 5 feet tall, with large, coarse, sticky leaves and long spikes of fragrant, white, tubular flowers 3 to 4 inches long and 1 inch across that open at night. The tall varieties of flowering tobacco work well near windows or at the back of a border. Compact varieties are excellent in beds, border fronts, or containers.

Culture. Seeds germinate, uncovered, in 10 to 15 days at 70° to 75°F/21° to 24°C. Plant in well-drained average soil. Space compact varieties 9 to 12 inches apart, taller varieties 24 inches apart. *N. sylvestris* readily reseeds it-

Nierembergia

self. Newer varieties of *N. alata* are widely available at nurseries as transplants. Tobacco budworm and aphids can be pests; for controls, see page 50.

NIEREMBERGIA
Cup flower
Solanaceae

Flowers in: Summer
Colors: Blue, white, and violet
Exposure: Sun; partial shade in hot-summer climates
Grows to: 4 to 15 inches
When to plant: Sow seeds indoors 8 to 10 weeks before last frost

Sprawling and mounded, cup flower is literally covered with bell-shaped flowers throughout summer. Grown in most areas as an annual, it is a perennial in mild-winter climates. The plants are self-branching, with delicate, threadlike, ½- to ⅔-inch-long leaves. They are effective edging beds, and their spreading, floriferous habit also suits them to use in window boxes or hanging baskets. *N. hippomanica*, known as dwarf cup flower, has white or pale blue flowers. *N. hippomanica violacea* (*N. h. caerulea*), the hardiest member of the genus, has purple flowers with yellow throats. It grows 6 to 15 inches tall. 'Purple Robe' has regal purple, golden-eyed, 1-inch blooms. *N. repens* forms a low-growing mat with white flowers.

Culture. Seeds germinate in 15 to 25 days at 70° to 75°F/21° to 24°C. Seedlings can withstand frost. Set out transplants 2 to 3 weeks before last frost. Plant 6 inches apart in average soil. Cut back after the first flush of flowers to prolong bloom. Plants grow best where summers are cool. Where summers are hot, provide water and shade.

Nigella damascena

NIGELLA DAMASCENA
Love-in-a-mist
Ranunculaceae

Flowers in: Spring
Colors: Blue, purple, pink, rose, and white
Exposure: Full sun or partial shade
Grows to: 18 to 24 inches
When to plant: Sow seeds outdoors in fall or early spring

Love-in-a-mist's name says it all. Charming, dainty cornflowerlike blooms are set within fine, feathery foliage, producing a misty show of pastel color. The flowers are followed by puffed-up, pale green seed capsules that add textural interest to dried arrangements. This plant is a beautiful companion to warm-colored dianthus or to poppies. It is not long-lived, and burns up in the heat of summer. The English Court series produces 2-inch-wide double blooms in white, light blue, rose-pink, and deep blue; the green seed pods are accented by prominent purple veins.

The less common *Nigella hispanica* 'Curiosity' has deep blue single flowers with dark centers and maroon stamens, borne on 24-inch plants.

Culture. Sow in well-drained ordinary soil. (For a longer bloom period, sow in fall and in early spring.) Seeds germinate in 7 to 14 days at 60°F/16°C. Thin to 6 to 8 inches apart. Transplanting is tricky. Plants will reseed themselves. To dry seed pods, cut branches when pods are mature and hang them upside down in an airy, shaded spot.

PAPAVER
Poppy
Papaveraceae

Flowers in: Spring through early summer
Colors: Shades of red, pink, orange, yellow, white, and bicolors
Exposure: Full sun
Grows to: 10 to 24 inches
When to plant: Sow seeds or set out transplants outdoors in fall or early spring

The Flanders Field poppy (*P. rhoeas*) or American Legion poppy is the antecedent of today's Shirley poppies, with their wide range of colors. This ancestor is a brilliant red poppy, with dark splotches at the base of the petals, that is grown in the open fields of western Europe. From it have been bred the numerous varieties of Shirley poppy, all bearing silky, translucent petals held in a cup shape. Flowers are 2 inches or more across, and are single or fully double; they dance above the foliage on slender, hairy stems. Leaves are pale green and deeply cut. 'Legion of Honor' has the brilliant crimson flowers and contrasting dark centers of the original form. The Mother of Pearl mix has flowers in delicate hues including gray, soft blue, lilac, peach, dusty pink, white, and speckled and picotee bicolors. All-Double Shirley is a mixture of 24-inch-tall plants with flowers in white, pink, rose, salmon, and scarlet.

Iceland poppy, *P. nudicaule*, is a perennial grown as an early-spring annual in mild-winter climates. It thrives in cool temperatures. The cup-

Papaver rhoeas

Pelargonium hortorum

shaped, slightly fragrant flowers are up to 3 or 4 inches across. The Wonderland series has giant 4-inch flowers on strong stems and grows to 10 inches tall. It is available in cream, white, orange, pink, and yellow. The Champagne Bubbles series produces strong, bushy, 12-inch-tall plants with flowers in a wide range of colors. The Sparkling Bubbles series includes pastel and other colors on 16-inch plants.

Culture. Sow in well-drained ordinary soil. In mild-winter climates, plant in early fall. Where winters are severe, wait until early spring. Because seeds are tiny, mix them with sand before broadcasting on the seedbed. Seeds germinate in 7 to 14 days. Thin to 6 to 12 inches apart. *P. rhoeas* has a short bloom period, and can be succession-sown in early spring in cool climates. Remove seed heads to prolong flowering. All *Papaver* species are excellent cut flowers; cut when flowers are in bud, and sear stem ends in boiling water or over a flame.

PELARGONIUM
Geranium
Geraniaceae

Flowers in: Spring, summer, fall
Colors: Shades of red, pink, orange, violet, white, and bicolors
Exposure: Full sun to partial shade, depending on variety
Grows to: 8 to 36 inches or more
When to plant: Set out transplants or rooted cuttings in spring

There is hardly any bedding plant as universally popular or well loved as the geranium. These South African natives are actually perennials, but are grown as annual bedding plants where winters are cold. Leaves are generally round or heart-shaped, with scalloped or fluted edges. Several species within the genus are grown as annuals.

Most commonly available, in a wide range of named varieties and easiest to grow, is the zonal geranium (*P. hortorum*). The common name comes from the darker zone of color ringing most leaves of the type. Its flower clusters are flat-topped and individual flowers are single or double. The plants are upright and bushy. With their floriferous nature, these plants are invaluable in patio containers and window boxes, and look especially attractive when mixed with petunias and sweet alyssum.

The ivy geranium (*P. peltatum*) has trailing stems up to 36 inches in length, making it ideal to cascade from hanging baskets. The flowers often have dark markings.

Scented geraniums are available in a variety of fragrances. The foliage carries the scent, which can be detected when a leaf is crushed or rubbed. Among the scented varieties are rose-scented (*P. graveolens*), lemon-scented (*P. crispum*), and peppermint-scented (*P. tomentosum*) kinds.

Of the zonal geraniums, the free-blooming Multibloom strain has a long flowering season and compact growth. Growing just 8 to 10 inches tall, it is suitable for mass plantings and is available in 8 colors. Elite is early to flower and has short stems holding well-rounded flower heads just above the foliage. Orbit is known for its ease of growing, uniformity of habit, and its large round flower heads. Available in 17 colors, it offers the widest color range of any geranium series. 'Orange Appeal' was bred for its appealing orange color. 'Hollywood Star' is among the best bicolors, with rose-and-white blossoms. 'Freckles', a 1991 All-America Selection, has a unique rose spot on the inside of each pink petal. Some cutting-grown zonal geraniums have variegated leaves—like 'Happy Thoughts', with its ball of red flowers atop predominantly white foliage edged in green, and 'Mrs. Parker', which has rose-pink florets above green leaves edged in white.

Of the ivy-leafed geraniums, 'Summer Showers' looks stunning in hanging baskets, with its cascading habit and loose red, pink, and white flower heads borne above foliage resembling that of English ivy. 'Breakaway Hybrid' was bred especially for hanging baskets; it has rounded pink and red flower heads 5 to 6 inches across.

Culture. It is convenient to purchase nursery-grown transplants, since growing from seeds takes a long time. Seeds germinate in 7 to 10 days at 70° to 75°F/21° to 24°C, but require 13 to 15 weeks to come into bloom.

When using zonal geraniums as bedding plants, set them 12 inches apart in fertile, well-drained soil. Keep plants pruned to the desired shape, using the cuttings to start new plants (cuttings root easily in water or moist sand and can then be planted outdoors).

For winter bloom, start young plants in summer and pinch off buds until the plants are brought indoors. For best indoor growth, keep in a sunny window in a relatively humid room (such as a kitchen or bathroom).

Zonal geraniums may also be lifted in fall and overwintered in a cool, unheated cellar. Brush off nearly all the soil from the roots and hang the plants upside down. In spring, cut back the withered stems to 6 to 8 inches and plant outdoors.

The ivy-leafed varieties prefer partial shade. They work well on patios and balconies.

Geranium budworm is a particularly troublesome pest in some areas. See page 50 for controls.

Pentzia

PENTZIA
Gold button
Compositae

Flowers in: Summer
Color: Orange
Exposure: Full sun
Grows to: 24 to 30 inches
When to plant: Sow seeds outdoors in early spring

An excellent cut flower for fresh or dried bouquets, gold button bears flattened globes of golden orange, ¾-inch-diameter flowers on dense, bushy plants. When dried, they hold their color indefinitely.

Culture. Broadcast seeds in average soil. *Pentzia* seeds germinate in 5 days at 70°F/21°C. Deadhead spent flowers to prolong bloom. To dry flowers, cut gold buttons when fully open and then hang them upside down in an airy but shaded spot.

PETUNIA HYBRIDA
Common garden petunia
Solanaceae

Flowers in: Late spring to fall
Colors: Shades of pink, red, salmon, coral, yellow, cream, blue, purple, white, and bicolors
Exposure: Full sun
Grows to: 8 to 27 inches
When to plant: Set out transplants in spring after all danger of frost is past

Petunias are valued for their large, richly colored flowers and long blooming period. They are suitable for edg-

Petunia hybrida

ing beds and borders, interplanting with annuals and perennials in mixed borders, and cultivation in containers or hanging baskets. The plants are adaptable to a wide range of soil and water conditions, and the delicately fragrant flowers are good for cutting. In warm-winter areas of the desert Southwest, petunias can be planted in fall to produce late-winter to mid-summer color.

Single flowers are trumpet-shaped. Double forms resemble carnations. Petunias are generally classed as Grandifloras (those with very large flowers, up to 4½ inches across) or Multifloras (numerous flowers, up to 2 inches across). Botrytis disease can damage blossoms and foliage in humid weather. Multifloras, with their numerous, smaller blossoms, recover more quickly after rainy periods. Hybrids are more expensive because they must be hand-pollinated, but are also more valuable because of their improved colors, uniform growth habits, and ability to stand up to heavy summer rains.

Among the hybrid single Grandifloras, the Ultra series offers extra-compact plants with a spreading habit, available in 13 colors, including the All-America Selection, 'Crimson Star'. The Frost strain, in red, wine-purple, and violet-blue, is eye-catching, with richly textured petals trimmed in white. The Cascade/Supercascade series, with its basal-branching, cascading habit, is excellent for hanging baskets and containers; it comes in 10 colors. The Daddy series has ruffled blooms with brightly colored veins. The Highlight series has a good tolerance to heavy rains but is more susceptible to botrytis disease; its 3-inch blooms are distinctively marked with white throats.

Single Multifloras include the Prime Time series, which is early, compact, and uniform, and is available in 15 colors, including bicolors starred with white. The Plum series has deep and lacy veining on the blossoms; it includes 'Summer Sun', the original true yellow petunia. The compact-growing Celebrity series has flowers in 11 colors, including some with deeply contrasting veins.

Among the double petunias, 'Circus' and 'Purple Pirouette' are both

Grandifloras and All-America Selections, the former with salmon-red and white bicolored blossoms, the latter with bright violet flowers edged in white. The Delight series of double Multifloras offers white, salmon, and red-and-white blossoms.

Culture. Plant in well-drained soil, spacing 7 to 10 inches apart. Because petunias are among the most popular annuals, nurseries carry a wide selection of varieties as young plants. Pinch developing plants to encourage bushy growth. Feed with a complete fertilizer each month, and deadhead regularly to promote continued flowering. As plants become leggy or straggly, cut back to encourage new growth. Smog can produce spots on the leaves of seedlings, especially white-flowered varieties. Tobacco budworm is a pest in some areas; see page 50 for control. Plants can be dug in fall before frost and brought indoors for winter color.

To grow petunias from seed, sow 8 to 10 weeks before last frost. Mix the seed with sand and broadcast on a moist growing medium. Germination takes 10 to 12 days at 70° to 80°F/21° to 27°C. Plants flower 2 to 2½ months from sowing.

PHLOX DRUMMONDII
Annual phlox, Texas pride
Polemoniaceae

Flowers in: Summer to fall
Colors: Red, pink, salmon, purple, white, and bicolors
Exposure: Full sun
Grows to: 6 to 20 inches
When to plant: Sow seeds outdoors after all danger of frost is past; sow in fall in mild-winter and desert climates

This Texas native bears clusters of colorful, slightly fragrant, 1-inch flowers (fine for cutting) atop erect, leafy stems. Bloom continues throughout summer. Dwarf varieties can serve as a flowering ground cover for summer-blooming bulbs. The Palona series is compact and floriferous, growing 8 to 10 inches tall. Available in carmine, crimson, rose, salmon, and white, plants perform well in both cool and moderate climates. The Petticoat strain has 6- to 8-inch-tall plants covered with

Phlox drummondii

star-shaped flowers in white, red, rose, salmon, or pink, with white highlights. Free-flowering 'Brilliant' grows to 20 inches, with white and rose-colored blossoms. The spreading Cecily strain is available in a range of bright colors, many with contrasting eyes.

Culture. Plant in fertile, well-drained soil. Seeds germinate in 10 to 15 days. Space 10 inches apart. Feed monthly with a balanced fertilizer and deadhead to prolong bloom. Cuttings root easily in moist sand or water. Branches of tall varieties can be pegged down to promote growth from lateral buds.

PORTULACA GRANDIFLORA
Moss rose
Portulacaceae

Flowers in: Early summer to frost
Colors: White, cream, yellow, orange, red, and pink
Exposure: Full sun
Grows to: 6 inches
When to plant: Sow seeds outdoors in spring or set out transplants in spring after all danger of frost is past

Portulaca is an old-fashioned favorite that flourishes in sunny, dry areas where few other plants will grow. Silky-petaled, roselike flowers cover the sprawling plants with brilliant

Portulaca grandiflora

color. The reddish, well-branched stems have a trailing habit, and the leaves are narrow, tubular, and succulent. Flowers open fully in sun and close in late afternoon. The plant is an excellent choice for rock gardens, containers, and hanging baskets. The Sundial series is free-flowering and early-blooming. The single flowers of the Wildfire strain are attractive cascading from hanging baskets. The double blossoms of the Afternoon Delight series stay open well into the evening.

Culture. Sow seed in well-drained soil, and keep soil moist until germination. Thin to 8 to 12 inches apart. (To sow indoors, start 6 to 8 weeks before last frost; expect germination in 10 to 14 days at 70° to 80°F/21° to 27°C.) Moss rose often reseeds itself.

PRIMULA
Primrose
Primulaceae

Flowers in: Spring; midwinter in mild-winter areas
Colors: White, pink, red, lavender, purple, blue, yellow, and orange
Exposure: Shade
Grows to: 6 to 18 inches
When to plant: Set out transplants in spring; in mild-winter climates, set out in early fall

Of the more than 600 species within the genus *Primula*, three are often grown as annuals.

The fairy primrose, *P. malacoides*, carries its pink, red, or white blossoms in tiers on slender stems rising from rosettes of soft, pale green oval leaves. The First Love strain has fragrant ¾-inch flowers on strong, wiry, 6- to 8-inch stems. It is a good choice for containers.

P. obconica has clusters of 1½- to 2-inch-wide blooms on long, hairy stems. Its leaves are large, rounded, and hairy (the tiny hairs can cause skin rashes). The Cantata series has flowers up to 2 inches across in a mixture of pearly shades of carmine, pink, blue, apricot, and lavender on bushy 7- to 8-inch plants. Seven separate colors are available in the Juno series. The free-flowering, 12-inch plants have small leaves and early blooms.

P. polyantha has 1- to 2-inch flowers carried in large clusters on stems 12 to 18 inches high. Oval, medium green leaves are pointed and form a rosette. The Pacific Giant series bears flowers up to 2¾ inches across on plants to 12 inches tall.

Culture. These plants cannot tolerate heat. Give them moist, fertile soil. They are difficult to grow from seed, so it is advisable to purchase nursery-grown transplants.

Primula

Proboscidea louisianica

PROBOSCIDEA LOUISIANICA
Unicorn plant, Devil's claw
Martyniaceae

Flowers in: Summer
Colors: Cream, lavender, and pink
Exposure: Full sun
Grows to: Sprawling, to 36 inches
When to plant: In long-summer areas, sow seeds outdoors in spring. In short-summer areas, sow seeds indoors 4 to 6 weeks before last frost

Unicorn plant is grown for its unusual claw-shaped seed pods, which, when dried, resemble birds' feet. It is native to the south central United States. The low, spreading plants have spikes of 2-inch-wide, bell-shaped flowers, the throats of which are blotched with purple or yellow. Leaves are round or heart-shaped, and both leaves and stems are covered with sticky hairs. The green seed pods resemble an elephant's trunk; when they ripen, they split into two or three parts, giving the pod its clawlike appearance. The plant gives off a musky scent that some consider unpleasant.

Culture. To improve germination, soak the seeds for 10 days to loosen seed coats. Seeds germinate in 2 to 8 weeks at 80° to 85°F/27° to 29°C. Plant in rich soil, 4 to 5 feet apart, some distance from other flower gardens (to accommodate the spreading growth habit and strong scent). It grows best in warm weather. To dry pods, cut stems with the pods attached, then hang upside down.

Reseda odorata

RESEDA ODORATA
Mignonette
Resedaceae

Flowers in: Spring
Colors: Greenish white tinged with copper or yellow
Exposure: Sun in cool climates; partial shade in warm climates
Grows to: 12 to 18 inches
When to plant: Sow seeds outdoors as soon as ground can be worked in spring; in mild-winter climates, sow outdoors in late fall or winter

Mignonette is grown for its extraordinarily sweet fragrance. The tiny flowers are borne in dense spikes that loosen as blossoms mature. Plants can be massed for an incredibly fragrant effect. Or interplant them with scentless plants to provide spots of fragrance. Beds or borders near windows and doorways can, in fair weather, perfume the indoors.

Machet, a Dutch strain, has plumes of fringed flowers 12 to 14 inches tall.

Culture. Mignonette grows best in cool weather; flowers dry quickly in heat. Broadcast seeds on the surface of fertile, well-worked soil. Seeds germinate in 2 to 3 weeks at 55°F/13°C. Thin to 10 inches apart. Provide regular, frequent watering. In suitable climates, succession sowing can prolong bloom.

Rudbeckia hirta

RUDBECKIA HIRTA
Black-eyed Susan, Gloriosa daisy
Compositae

Flowers in: Summer
Colors: Yellow, gold, mahogany red, and bicolors
Exposure: Full sun or light shade
Grows to: 8 to 36 inches
When to plant: Sow seeds outdoors in fall or early spring

Easily grown, black-eyed Susans have single or double daisylike flowers; yellow petals surround purplish-brown centers. They flower well in the heat of summer. The plants are short-lived perennials grown as half-hardy annuals. Flowers last well when cut, and cutting promotes continued bloom.

'Double Gold' produces double and semidouble 4½-inch flowers with golden yellow petals and deep brown eyes on 36-inch-tall plants. 'Goldilocks' grows just 8 to 10 inches tall, with double and semidouble blooms of bright gold on compact plants. The hybrid Gloriosa Daisy strain produces flowers up to 6 inches across in shades of yellow, gold, reddish brown, and bicolors, on 36-inch plants. 'Irish Eyes' has 4½- to 5-inch single flowers with yellow petals and unusual clear green centers on 30-inch plants.

Culture. Plant in ordinary soil. Seeds germinate in 14 days. Thin to 12 to 14 inches apart. It often reseeds itself.

SALPIGLOSSIS SINUATA
Painted-tongue, Velvet flower
Solanaceae

Flowers in: Late spring and early summer
Colors: White, yellow, red, pink, purple, and brown
Exposure: Full sun
Grows to: 12 to 36 inches
When to plant: Sow seeds indoors 6 to 8 weeks before last frost

Most successful where summers are cool, painted-tongue provides a brilliant display in beds and borders. The trumpet-shaped flowers have an unusual combination of velvety texture; muted, rich colors; and delicate vein-

Salpiglossis sinuata

ing. They are held in loose clusters on slender, wiry stems. The sticky foliage is lance-shaped and widely notched. Painted-tongue is a good choice for the middle of a border and is complemented by baby's breath or love-in-a-mist. The cut flowers add color, depth, and formal interest to bouquets. Hybrid Casino mixture has a branching habit ideal for bedding, containers, and cutting, and grows 18 to 24 inches tall. 'Kew Blue' grows 12 inches tall, with rich blue flowers accented by striking gold veins.

Culture. Plant seeds in peat pots in a warm, protected location (70° to 80°F/ 21° to 27°C); expect germination in 7 to 10 days. Plant out 12 inches apart in average soil after all danger of frost is past. Pinch young plants to promote bushy growth. Stake taller varieties to keep them upright. The plant is perennial in mild-winter climates.

SALVIA
Sage
Labiatae

Flowers in: Early summer to frost
Colors: Blue, lavender, purple, red, coral, and white
Exposure: Full sun or partial shade
Grows to: 8 to 36 inches
When to plant: Sow seeds indoors 4 to 6 weeks before last frost

Salvia farinacea

The *Salvia* genus includes a number of perennials, such as culinary sage, and tender annuals. *S. farinacea*, mealy-cup sage, is a perennial grown as an annual in cold-winter climates. Its flowers are carried in tiers on tall, slender stems. Each ½-inch-long blossom is held in a calyx covered with short, whitish hairs, giving the plant a mealy appearance. Silvery foliage forms a mound at the base of the plant. Flowers are good for cutting. The Victoria series has compact 18- to 20-inch plants with medium blue or silvery white flowers. It flowers over a long period and is effective planted in masses.

Gentian sage (*S. patens*) grows to 36 inches tall. The arrow-shaped, 2- to 5-inch-long leaves are covered with short, sticky hairs. Small tubular flowers hang from tall stems. It is evergreen in mild climates, but grown as an annual where winters are severe.

The flowers of *S. viridis* (*S. horminum*), a tender annual, are insignificant, but the leaflike bracts at the top of the plant are colored pink, white, or blue and look attractive in fresh and dried arrangements. 'Claryssa' grows to 18 inches tall with a compact habit.

Scarlet sage (*S. splendens*) has spikes of vividly colored 1½-inch-long tubular flowers that are surrounded by equally colorful calyxes. It will grow well in light shade, especially in hot-summer areas. The flowers do not last long when cut. Their bright colors combine well with white sweet alyssum or silvery dusty miller. The blossoms are attractive to hummingbirds. In addition to the original scarlet color, shades of salmon, lilac, purple, and white are available in both the Empire and Hotline series. 'Red-Hot Sally' has deep red blooms on 10-inch plants. Medium-tall 'Flare' has 18-inch-long red spikes, while 'Bonfire' grows bright red spikes up to 26 inches tall. 'Melba' produces salmon-coral flowers with lighter tips on 8-inch plants.

Culture. Sow seeds on a moist planting medium, with germination in 12 to 15 days at 70°F/21°C (soak seeds of *S. splendens* to speed germination). Plant out after all danger of frost is past. Space 12 inches apart. Water often and feed monthly to keep plants vigorous.

SANVITALIA PROCUMBENS
Creeping zinnia
Compositae

Flowers in: Summer to fall
Colors: Orange, yellow, or white, with purplish brown centers
Exposure: Sun
Grows to: 6 to 8 inches
When to plant: Sow seeds outdoors in spring after the danger of frost is past

The tiny, bright, zinnialike flowers and trailing habit of creeping zinnia make it attractive as an edging for a border, clumped in a rock garden, or cascading from a window box or hanging basket. Masses of small single or double flowers with warm-colored petals and purple or brown centers bloom until frost. Dark green leaves are oval and pointed. 'Mandarin Orange' has vivid orange blooms with dark eyes. The ½- to ¾-inch-wide flowers cover creeping plants that grow 8 inches high and spread up to 16 inches across. 'Gold Braid' has fully double gold blossoms.

Culture. Sow in light, well-drained soil, leaving the seeds uncovered. Seeds germinate in 1 to 2 weeks at 68°F/20°C. Thin to 3 inches apart. Plants thrive in heat and with a minimum of water, once established. However, if allowed to go completely dry, creeping zinnia will stop blooming.

Sanvitalia procumbens

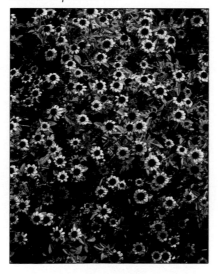

Scabiosa atropurpurea

SCABIOSA ATROPURPUREA
Pincushion flower, Sweet scabious
Dipsaceae

Flowers in: Summer to fall
Colors: White, pink, salmon, red, maroon, lavender, purple, and blue
Exposure: Full sun
Grows to: 24 to 36 inches
When to plant: Sow seeds outdoors in spring; sow in fall in mild-winter climates

Pincushion flower gets its name from the light-colored stamens that protrude from each of many tiny flowers clustered together in a mound; these look like pins stuck into the flower. The 2-inch-wide flower heads rise above a rosette of slender, coarsely toothed leaves. Sweetly fragrant flowers are followed by pale green, cupped seed pods that are covered with bristly reddish hairs, resembling a bottle brush. The Imperial Giants strain includes a deep maroon-purple color that is unusual among annuals, as well as pink, white, salmon, scarlet, deep rose, red, lavender, and blue. *S. stellata* is an annual from southern Europe that is grown for its unusual seed pods; spherical light blue or white flowers turn into papery bronze seed heads of complex design, carried on 6- to 18-inch stems. 'Ping Pong' has small white flowers that are followed by intricate seed heads, each segment centered by a delicate maroon star. The seed heads provide unique accents in dried arrangements.

Culture. Sow in average, well-drained soil. Seeds germinate in 10 to 12 days. Thin to 6 to 8 inches apart. Plants flower best in climates with moderate summer temperatures.

Schizanthus pinnatus

SCHIZANTHUS PINNATUS
**Butterfly flower,
Poor man's orchid**
Solanaceae

Flowers in: Summer; winter and spring in mild-winter climates
Colors: Pink, red, violet, purple, yellow, and white
Exposure: Filtered shade
Grows to: 6 to 24 inches
When to plant: Sow seeds outdoors in spring; in mild-winter climates, sow outdoors in fall

The brilliant, orchidlike blossoms of butterfly flower provide an effective display in containers or at the front of a border. It is best grown in cool-summer areas, and is attractive planted with *Primula malacoides* and cineraria, which flourish in the same climates. Gold-veined flowers cluster on slender, cascading stems. They last well as cut flowers. Dainty fernlike foliage is inconspicuous compared with the blossoms.

The Star Parade strain provides ball-shaped plants that grow 8 inches across and are covered with purple-to-yellow flowers. The Angel Wings strain grows 12 inches high and spreads 10 inches across, with light pink, salmon, carmine, scarlet, lilac; and purple flowers.

Culture. Sow in moist soil. Seeds germinate in 7 to 14 days at 60° to 70°F/ 16° to 21°C. Thin to 12 inches apart. The flowering season is short, but can be extended by succession sowing. Stake taller varieties to keep upright.

SENECIO HYBRIDUS
Cineraria
Compositae

Flowers in: Spring and early summer; late winter and early spring in mild-winter climates
Colors: White, pink, red, yellow, blue, and purple
Exposure: Shade
Grows to: 12 to 15 inches
When to plant: Set out transplants in spring; in mild-winter climates, plant out in fall

Cineraria thrives in cool-summer climates, where its bright colors can light up a shady garden. Velvety flowers, some with contrasting eyes, are held in domed clusters 3 to 5 inches across. The lush green leaves are rounded or heart-shaped, with wavy or toothed margins. The Improved Festival Grandiflora strain produces free-flowering 12- to 14-inch plants with solid and bicolor blooms with distinct eyes. The Multiflora Starlet strain is a compact 8 to 10 inches tall, with florets in red, crimson, copper, rose, white, yellow, and dark and light blue, some with eyes ringed in white.

Culture. Cineraria takes several months to flower from seed, and is most easily grown from purchased transplants. Plant in cool, moist, fertile soil. Water regularly, never letting the plant dry out. Leaf miners, spider mites, slugs, and snails can be problems; for controls, see pages 50–51. Although cineraria is perennial in mild-winter climates, start with new plants each season to get the best

Senecio hybridus

Tagetes

bloom. Plants reseed themselves where the climate suits them. Seeds germinate, uncovered, in 10 to 14 days at 70° to 75°F/21° to 24°C.

TAGETES
Marigold
Compositae

Flowers in: Early summer until frost
Colors: White, off-white, yellow, orange, and orange-red
Exposure: Full sun
Grows to: 6 inches to 4 feet
When to plant: Sow seeds outdoors or set out transplants in spring, after all danger of frost is past

Marigolds are among the most popular flowers in American gardens, producing vibrant color, flowering quickly from seed, and continuing to bloom through the heat of summer. Gardeners today have a wide assortment of marigolds from which to choose, with flowers in almost all the tints and tones of orange and yellow and a good measure of reds, and in many combinations. Flowers come in a pleasing variety of shapes, from single to fully double, and rise well above the foliage. All have vivid beauty and long life when cut. The plants are sturdy and well branched, with attractive, rather finely cut, dark green foliage. The yellow-tinted marigolds fit into any garden design, whether a soft-hued bed or a brilliant color scheme. Use the orange shades more carefully. Most marigolds have a sharp fragrance, but several of the new hybrids have foliage and flowers with no scent.

For use in cut arrangements, strip away most of the foliage from the stems to reduce the pungent scent.

All garden marigolds descend from Mexican species that have been developed and hybridized to produce four separate types. The African, or American, marigold (*Tagetes erecta*) has huge blossoms, 3½ to 5 inches across, on plants that grow 20 to 36 inches tall. Colors, all single, include rich glowing orange, lemon-gold, and sulphur-yellow. The chrysanthemum-flowered varieties have globe-shaped double blooms; carnation-flowered varieties are densely double, with petals waved and rolled. The Perfection series is unsurpassed for mass planting, with a unique petal structure providing weather tolerance. 'Snowdrift' is the best white marigold. The Discovery series has compact plants with super-large, ball-shaped flowers.

So-called French marigolds (*Tagetes patula*) are low-growing (7 to 10 inches), with 1- to 2-inch single or double flowers in many shades of yellow, orange, copper, mahogany red, and combinations. The French marigolds are ideal for foregrounds, bedding, edging, window boxes and other containers, and in small bouquets. As the nights cool, they redouble their efforts, and each individual plant becomes a bouquet in itself. The Boy series, although small-flowered, produces masses of very early blooms with crested centers. The Aurora series offers fully double, compact good looks and dependability, and the new 'Aurora Yellow Fire' presents an unusual color combination of bright yellow and mahogany red. The Janie series has crested flowers with a shapely silhouette; it's the earliest and most floriferous of the French marigolds.

Although French marigolds have long been recommended for nematode control, recent university studies have not confirmed this relationship.

Triploid hybrids are crosses between African and French marigolds, combining African vigor and compact French habit. They bloom early, and because they are unable to set seed, produce scores of 2- to 3-inch blossoms. The Nugget Supreme series offers better germination than others in the class.

Signet or Mexican marigolds (*Tagetes signata pumila*, also known as *T. tenuifolia pumila*) have dainty single flowers. The dwarf, bushy plants feature lacy, fernlike foliage with a delightful lemon fragrance, and are ideal for edging. The flowers are tiny, usually less than 1 inch across, but borne so profusely as to make the plants a solid mass of color for many weeks. The Gem series is available in gold and lemon-yellow. Paprika has bright pimento-red petals edged in gold.

Culture. Marigolds flourish in ordinary garden soil in full sun (be careful not to overfertilize or plant in soil that is very rich in nitrogen, which will produce foliage at the expense of flowers). Seeds are quite large and should be planted ¼ inch deep. They will germinate in about 7 days at 75° to 80°F/24° to 27°C. For extra-early flowers, start seeds 5 or 6 weeks before you set them out, and transfer seedlings to flats or pots as soon as true leaves have formed. Plant outside after the soil has warmed. Space taller varieties 12 to 24 inches apart, dwarf varieties about 6 inches apart. Stake taller varieties early. Remove spent blossoms regularly to encourage continuous flowering.

TALINUM PANICULATUM
Jewels of Opar
Portulacaceae

Flowers in: Summer
Colors: Rosy pink
Exposure: Sun
Grows to: 24 to 30 inches
When to plant: Sow seeds indoors 6 to 8 weeks before last frost

With its airy panicles of tiny blossoms, Jewels of Opar provides a delightful

Talinum paniculatum

Thunbergia

filler for cut flower arrangements. The dense, well-branched plants are covered in glossy, dark green foliage. The blooms, which last only a day, are borne in rapid succession through summer heat and drought.

Culture. Seeds germinate in 5 to 20 days at 68°F/20°C. Plant out in average soil. Space 12 inches apart.

THUNBERGIA ALATA
Black-eyed Susan vine
Acanthaceae

Flowers in: Summer
Colors: White, yellow, and orange
Exposure: Full sun or light shade
Grows to: Climber, up to 10 feet
When to plant: Sow seeds indoors 6 to 8 weeks before last frost

The twining black-eyed Susan vine is studded with flaring 1-inch-diameter tubular flowers. Bright green triangular leaves are 3 inches long. A perennial in mild-winter climates, it is widely grown as a summer annual. The dark-eyed blossoms look decorative on fences and trellises, and dwarf forms are attractive trailing from hanging baskets and window boxes. The Susie series produces vines up to 5 feet long and flowers 1 to 2 inches across. It is a good choice for hanging baskets. *T. gregorii* is similar, without the dark eye in the flower.

Culture. Seeds germinate in 14 to 21 days at 70° to 75°F/21° to 24°C. Set out plants in moist, fertile soil after weather has warmed. Space 12 inches apart.

Tithonia rotundifolia

TITHONIA ROTUNDIFOLIA
Mexican sunflower
Compositae

Flowers in: Summer
Colors: Orange with yellow-orange centers
Exposure: Full sun
Grows to: 30 inches to 5 feet
When to plant: Sow seeds indoors 6 weeks before last frost

The glowing orange, daisylike blooms of Mexican sunflower grow profusely on large, somewhat coarse plants; faintly fragrant, the 3-inch flowers attract butterflies. Deeply veined dark green leaves have serrated edges. Plants grow quickly and may be used as a temporary hedge. Mexican sunflower is heat resistant, and is a good selection for a desert garden. The flowers are handsome when cut. 'Goldfinger' grows 30 to 42 inches tall. Aphids can be a pest; for controls, see page 50.

Culture. Seeds germinate in 10 to 18 days at 70° to 80°F/21° to 27°C. Transplant after all danger of frost is past. Plant in ordinary soil. Space 24 inches apart. Stake to maintain upright habit. Flowers bloom 2 to 3 months after sowing. For cut flowers, sear stem ends in boiling water or over a flame, and condition in warm water.

Torenia fournieri

TORENIA FOURNIERI
Wishbone flower
Scrophulariaceae

Flowers in: Summer to fall
Colors: Blue, lavender, violet, red, pink, and white
Exposure: Partial shade; in sun in cool-summer climates
Grows to: 6 to 12 inches
When to plant: Sow seeds indoors 6 to 8 weeks before last frost

Wishbone flower has small blossoms up to 1 inch across; they resemble miniature gloxinias. The common name comes from the wishbone shape of the stamen in the center of the blossom. Flower petals are often blotched with a contrasting color. Attractive in containers, this plant can also be used as an edging for beds and borders. Lift during fall for indoor bloom. The Clown strain, an All-America Selection, blooms 10 to 14 days earlier than other strains; its globe-shaped plants, which grow 6 to 8 inches tall, produce blooms in white, light blue, dark blue, and rose-pink.

Culture. Seeds germinate, uncovered, in 7 to 15 days at 70°F/21°C. Set out transplants after all danger of frost is past. Plant in moist, fertile soil. Keep watered well. Pinch to promote bushy growth.

TRACHYMENE COERULEA
Blue lace flower
Umbelliferae

Flowers in: Spring; summer in cool-summer climates
Colors: Blue
Exposure: Full sun
Grows to: 24 inches
When to plant: Sow seeds outdoors in spring

Blooms consist of numerous small, sweet-scented, pale blue flowers clustered together in flat-topped umbels. Hairy, much-divided leaves add to the lacy effect. The plant is not particularly showy in garden beds, but is excellent for cutting.

Culture. Sow seeds in average soil. Seeds germinate in 2 to 3 weeks at

Trachymene coerulea

68°F/20°C. Water frequently and provide support for young plants. Blue lace flower is best suited to cool-summer areas.

TROPAEOLUM MAJUS
Nasturtium
Tropaeolaceae

Flowers in: Summer; winter to spring in warm-winter climates
Colors: Cream, yellow, orange, red, and pink
Exposure: Full sun
Grows to: Dwarfs to 15 inches, climbers to 6 to 10 feet
When to plant: Sow seeds outdoors in spring after all danger of frost is past; in mild-winter climates, sow seeds outdoors in fall

Gardeners love nasturtiums for their attractive round foliage and plentiful flowers. Blooms are held on slender stems growing from the axils of the leaves; newer varieties hold the spurred flowers well above the foliage. Young leaves and blossoms have a peppery flavor and are colorful additions in salads. Dwarf varieties are good edging plants for flower and vegetable beds. Climbing varieties may be used to cover trellises or as a ground cover and are also attractive trailing from hanging baskets and window boxes. The Alaska strain has variegated foliage, small leaves, and blooms in cream, yellow, gold, orange, scarlet, mahogany, rose, pink, and apricot on 12- to 15-inch plants. The Whirlybird series has upward-facing flowers on nearly vertical stems. The midsize Double Gleam series, an All-America Selection, has large, fragrant double and semidouble flowers on 36-inch plants. 'Empress of India' has blue-green leaves and single vermilion flowers on 12-inch plants.

Tropaeolum majus

Canary bird flower (*T. peregrinum*) is a climber growing 10 to 15 feet. Its small yellow flowers have feathery petals. It grows best in cool-summer climates and requires moist soil.

Culture. Plant in average, well-drained soil (rich soil will produce excess foliage at the expense of flowers). Seeds germinate in 14 days. Thin to 12 inches apart. Nasturtiums will live over in mild-winter climates and often reseed themselves. They flower best in cool weather and do not grow well in extremely hot, humid weather. They do not transplant well. Aphids and mealybugs are common pests. For controls, see page 50.

VERBENA HYBRIDA
Garden verbena, Vervain
Verbenaceae

Flowers in: Summer to fall
Colors: White, pink, bright red, purple, blue, and bicolors
Exposure: Full sun
Grows to: 6 to 12 inches
When to plant: Sow seeds indoors 6 to 8 weeks before last frost

Verbena is an old-fashioned favorite among annuals. Its small, richly colored, fragrant flowers are borne in flat clusters 2 to 3 inches wide. The well-branched plants are available in

Verbena hybrida

mounded, trailing, and dwarf forms. Broad, lance-shaped, medium- to gray-green leaves have serrated edges. When in full bloom, plants are a solid mass of color. They are attractive grouped in a border. The trailing forms are useful to create a flowering ground cover and are good choices for hanging baskets. The Amour series has an upright habit and is early to flower. Large, ball-shaped flower heads come in pink, red, purple, white, and rose as well as a mix that includes additional colors. The Springtime series is suitable for hanging baskets and as a ground cover. The Romance strain grows 8 to 10 inches tall, with flowers in scarlet, white, and a mixture. The Showtime series spreads to 18 inches across, in a blend of red, white, violet-blue, rose, and pink. 'Trinidad' has vibrant rose flowers on 10-inch plants. 'Valentine' has clusters of scarlet red blooms with white eyes, up to 3 inches across, on 15-inch plants.

Culture. Chill the seeds 1 week before sowing. Surface-sow on a moistened growing medium. Cover with black plastic until germination begins. Seeds germinate in 3 to 4 weeks at 50° to 75°F/10° to 24°C. Set out transplants after all danger of frost is past. Space 12 to 18 inches apart. Pinch back young plants to promote bushy growth. Deadhead to prolong flowering. Plants can be cut back after the first flush of bloom to encourage fall flower production. Plants may live over in mild-winter climates, but old plants are inferior in growth and flower habit. Verbena is susceptible to rot from excessive moisture.

VIOLA
Pansy, Viola
Violaceae

Flowers in: Early spring to early summer; late winter and spring in mild-winter climates
Colors: White, yellow, orange, red, purple, blue, and bicolors
Exposure: Full sun or partial shade
Grows to: 8 inches
When to plant: Set out transplants several weeks before last frost; in mild-winter climates, set out plants in summer and fall

Viola

The happy faces of low-growing pansies provide brilliant color in cool-season gardens. They are popular for massing with spring-blooming bulbs, and are suitable for containers, hanging baskets, and rock gardens. The velvety flowers of pansies (*V. wittrockiana*) and violas are 2 to 5 inches across and made up of five overlapping petals. They are available in single colors and with contrasting splotches, brightly colored centers, and markings resembling whiskers. Cut flowers make charming small bouquets. Leaves are heart-shaped or oval, sometimes deeply lobed.

The heat-tolerant Crystal Bowl series has 2-inch flowers in 11 clear colors. 'Delft' has 2-inch blooms of porcelain blue and white marked with whiskers and contrasting bright yellow eyes. The Majestic Giant series has huge 4-inch flowers with dark blotches on early-blooming plants, available in 6 colors. The Maxim strain includes All-America Selection 'Maxim Marina', with light blue petals surrounding a dark blue face bordered in white; it resists both heat and cold. 'Padparadja', an All-America Selection, has 2-inch flowers in a unique, clear orange color. The Universal series has a compact, mounded habit, with masses of bloom in 13 colors.

Violas (*V. cornuta*) are short-lived perennials best grown as annuals. The plants grow 8 to 10 inches tall, with flowers 1½ inches across. They are sometimes called horned violets because of the flowers' slender spurs. Their floriferous nature makes up for their smaller flowers, creating a delicate yet colorful show.

Johnny-jump-up (*V. tricolor*) has smaller flowers in a narrower range of colors—usually purple and yellow. They often reseed themselves.

(Continued on next page)

Culture. Pansies and violas must be started 10 weeks before planting out, and so are best purchased as nursery-grown transplants. Alternatively, in cold-winter climates, seeds can be sown in fall in a coldframe and seedlings transplanted in early spring. Seeds germinate in 10 to 21 days at 65° to 70°F/18° to 21°C. Plant in moist, fertile soil; mulch to keep cool and retain moisture. Pansies and violas are most floriferous when nights are cool. Deadhead and cut back leggy plants to prolong bloom. Even heat-tolerant varieties must be replaced in hot-summer climates.

ZINNIA ELEGANS
Garden zinnia
Compositae

Flowers in: Summer to fall
Colors: Shades of white, yellow, orange, red, pink, purple, and bicolors
Exposure: Full sun
Grows to: 6 to 36 inches
When to plant: Sow seeds outdoors in spring, or set out transplants in spring after all danger of frost is past

Zinnias are ever-popular annuals. Easily grown, the plants are available in many heights, flower forms, and colors. They bloom through the heat of summer and provide color in late summer, when most other annuals have finished. These multipurpose plants provide a showy display when massed, and lend color strength when mixed with annuals and perennials in borders.

Dwarf varieties make a colorful edging. The Thumbelina strain has charming small flowers on 6-inch plants. The Short Stuff series produces fully double blooms on 8- to 10-inch plants. The Dreamland series has blooms 4 inches across on 10- to 12-inch plants. 'Rose Pinwheel', bearing rose-pink flowers with yellow centers on 12-inch plants, was bred for mildew resistance. The Peter Pan strain begins to flower when plants are just 6 to 8 inches tall and continues all summer, maturing at a height of 12 to 14 inches. The Border Beauty series has dahlia-type double to semidouble flowers on bushy plants. The Candy

Zinnia Dreamland

Cane series has bright pink, rose, and cerise stripes on white petals, and grows to 17 inches. Hybrid 'Small World Cherry' is an All-America Selection, and one of the most vigorous of all zinnias. The Lilliput strain has vivid, pompon-type blooms on 18- to 24-inch tall plants. Flowers of the Ruffles hybrid series are borne on 24- to 30-inch stems. 'Scarlet Splendor' has

rich, 4- to 5-inch scarlet flowers with semiruffled petals; the plants have a hedgelike habit and require less space than other tall varieties.

Z. angustifolia has compact plants with narrow leaves and flowers 1 inch across; it often lives over in mild-winter climates. 'Classic', with its 1½-inch-wide orange flowers, and 'Classic White', a white-flowering counterpart, have spreading habits and make good choices for hanging baskets. The Persian Carpet strain and 'Old Mexico' variety of *Z. haageana* produce 1½-inch-wide double and semidouble flowers in bright shades of brownish red, yellow, and orange, with pointed petals tipped or bordered with a contrasting color. They are an especially attractive and free-blooming edging.

Culture. Sow in average soil, after it has warmed. Seeds germinate in 7 to 10 days at 70° to 80°F/21° to 27°C. Thin seedlings to 6 to 12 inches apart. Deadhead flowers to prolong bloom. Ground-level watering will help prevent mildew, to which zinnias are susceptible. Feed monthly during the growing season with a complete fertilizer to encourage vigorous growth.

Seed Sources

Seeds of many annuals are sold in nurseries and garden centers. Mail-order catalogs, of which there are many, usually offer a wider selection. Here are three popular mail-order seed companies that offer a large variety of flowering annuals in free catalogs.

W. Atlee Burpee & Co.
300 Park Avenue
Warminster, PA 18974

Park Seed Company
Cokesbury Road
Greenwood, SC 29647-0001

Thompson & Morgan
P.O. Box 1308
Jackson, NJ 08527

Wildflowers

Index

Abelmoschus moschatus, 54
Acroclinium roseum. See
    Helipterum roseum, 76
African daisy. See Arctotis, 58;
    Dimorphotheca, 70
Ageratum houstonianum, 54
Alcea rosea, 55
All-America selections, 7
Althaea rosea. See Alcea rosea,
    55
Amaranthus, 55
Amethyst flower. See Browallia
    speciosa, 59
Ammi majus, 55
Ammobium alatum, 56
Anchusa capensis, 56
Annual baby's breath. See
    Gypsophila elegans, 74
Annual coreopsis. See
    Coreopsis tinctoria, 67
Annual delphinium. See
    Consolida ambigua, 66
Annual grasses, 56
Annual phlox. See Phlox
    drummondii, 86
Annuals
    color (by season), 14–19
    with colorful foliage, 30
    for containers, 24–25
    cool-season, 6
    for cut flowers, 28–29
    defined, 6–7
    designing with, 10–11, 12–13
    for dried bouquets, 32
    for edgings, 27
    fragrant, 33
    for hanging baskets, 26
    naturalizing, 34–35
    planting locations, 20–23, 27,
        38
    for shade, 22
    for sun, 20–21, 23
    tall, 31
    warm-season, 6
Antirrhinum majus, 57
Aphids, 50
Arctotis, 58

Baby blue eyes. See Nemophila,
    83
Baby's breath, annual. See
    Gypsophila elegans, 74
Bedding begonia. See Begonia
    sempervirens, 58
Beetles, 50
Begonia sempervirens, 58
Bells-of-Ireland. See Moluccella
    laevis, 82
Bird's eyes. See Gilia, 73
Bishop's flower. See Ammi
    majus, 55
Black-eyed Susan. See
    Rudbeckia hirta, 88

Black-eyed Susan vine. See
    Thunbergia alata, 91
Blanket flower. See Gaillardia
    pulchella, 72
Blue daisy. See Felicia, 72
Blue lace flower. See
    Trachymene coerulea, 92
Blue marguerite. See Felicia, 72
Blue thimble flower. See Gilia,
    73
Brachycome iberidifolia, 58
Brassica, 59
Browallia speciosa, 59
Bugloss. See Anchusa
    capensis, 56
Bupleurum griffithii, 60
Burning bush. See Kochia
    scoparia, 70
Busy Lizzy. See Impatiens, 76
Butterfly flower. See
    Schizanthus pinnatus, 90

Calceolaria, 60
Calendula officinalis, 60
California poppy. See
    Eschscholzia californica, 71
Calliopsis. See Coreopsis
    tinctoria, 67
Callistephus chinensis, 61
Campanula medium, 61
Candytuft. See Iberis, 76
Canterbury bells. See Cam-
    panula medium, 61
Cape forget-me-not. See
    Anchusa capensis, 56
Cape marigold. See
    Dimorphotheca, 70
Capsicum annuum, 62
Carnation. See Dianthus, 69
Carthamus tinctorius, 62
Catharanthus roseus, 62
Celosia argentea, 63
Centaurea, 63
Cheiranthus cheiri, 64
Cherry pie. See Heliotropium
    arborescens, 75
China aster. See Callistephus
    chinensis, 61
Chinese forget-me-not. See
    Cynoglossum amabile, 68
Chinese woolflower. See
    Celosia argentea, 63
Christmas pepper. See
    Capsicum annuum, 62
Chrysanthemum, 64
Cigar plant. See Cuphea ignea,
    68
Cineraria. See Senecio hybridus,
    90
Clarkia, 65
Cleome hasslerana, 65
Cockscomb. See Celosia
    argentea, 63

Coleus hybridus, 66
Colorful foliage, annuals with, 30
Color, garden
    designing with, 12–13
    in fall, 18
    by season, 14–19
    in spring, 14–15
    in summer, 16–17
    in winter, 19
Color wheel, 12–13
Common garden petunia. See
    Petunia hybrida, 85
Consolida ambigua, 66
Containers
    choices for, 24–25
    growing annuals in, 49
    planting from, 42
Convolvulus tricolor, 67
Cool-season annuals, 6
Coreopsis tinctoria, 67
Cornflower. See Centaurea, 63
Cosmos, 67
Creeping zinnia. See Sanvitalia
    procumbens, 89
Crepis rubra, 68
Cup flower. See Nierembergia,
    83
Cuphea ignea, 68
Cut flowers, annuals for, 28–29
Cynoglossum amabile, 68

Dahlberg daisy. See Dyssodia
    tenuiloba, 71
Dahlia, 69
Deadheading, 48
Delphinium ajacis. See
    Consolida ambigua, 66
Design, garden
    basics of, 10–11
    using color in, 12–13
Devil's claw. See Proboscidea
    louisianica, 87
Dianthus, 69
Diascia barberae, 70
Dimorphotheca, 70
Diseases, 50–51
Dried bouquets, annuals for, 32
Dusty miller. See Centaurea, 63
Dwarf morning glory. See
    Convolvulus tricolor, 67
Dyssodia tenuiloba, 71

Earwigs, 50
Edgings, annuals for, 27
Eschscholzia californica, 71
Euphorbia marginata, 71

False saffron. See Carthamus
    tinctorius, 62
Felicia, 72
Fertilizers, 46-47
Firecracker plant. See Cuphea
    ignea, 68

Five spot. See Nemophila, 83
Floss flower. See Ageratum
    houstonianum, 54
Flowering cabbage. See
    Brassica, 59
Flowering flax. See Linum
    grandiflorum, 79
Flowering kale. See Brassica, 59
Flowering tobacco. See
    Nicotiana, 83
Forget-me-not. See Myosotis
    sylvatica, 82
Four o'clock. See Mirabilis
    jalapa, 81
Fragrant annuals, 33

Gaillardia pulchella, 72
Garden balsam. See Impatiens,
    76
Garden verbena. See Verbena
    hybrida, 93
Garden zinnia. See Zinnia
    elegans, 94
Gazania rigens, 72
Geranium. See Pelargonium, 84
Geranium budworms, 50
Gerbera jamesonii, 73
Gilia, 73
Globe amaranth. See
    Gomphrena, 74
Gloriosa daisy. See Rudbeckia
    hirta, 88
Gold button. See Pentzia, 85
Golden fleece. See Dyssodia
    tenuiloba, 71
Gomphrena, 74
Grasses, annual, 56
Gypsophila elegans, 74

Hanging baskets, growing
    annuals in, 49
    choices for, 26
Hard-frost dates, 39
Hawk's beard. See Crepis
    rubra, 68
Helianthus annuus, 74
Helichrysum bracteatum, 75
Heliotrope. See Heliotropium
    arborescens, 75
Heliotropium arborescens, 75
Helipterum roseum, 76
Hollyhock. See Alcea rosea, 55

Iberis, 76
Impatiens, 76
Insect pests, 50–51
Ipomoea tricolor, 77

Jewels of Opar. See Talinum
    paniculatum, 91

Kingfisher daisy. See Felicia, 72
Kochia scoparia, 78

Larkspur. *See Consolida ambigua*, 66
Lathyrus odoratus, 78
Lavatera trimestris, 79
Limonium sinuatum, 79
Linaria maroccana, 79
Linum grandiflorum, 79
Lobelia erinus, 80
Lobularia maritima, 80
Love-in-a-mist. *See Nigella damascena*, 84
Love-lies-bleeding. *See Amaranthus*, 55
Lovely browallia. *See Browallia speciosa*, 59
Lychnis coeli-rosa, 80

Madagascar periwinkle. *See Catharanthus roseus*, 62
Maintenance, garden, 48
Marigold. *See Tagetes*, 90
Marvel of Peru. *See Mirabilis jalapa*, 81
Matthiola, 81
Mexican sunflower. *See Tithonia rotundifolia*, 92
Mignonette. *See Reseda odorata*, 88
Mimulus, 81
Mirabilis jalapa, 81
Mites, 51
Moluccella laevis, 82
Monkey flower. *See Mimulus*, 81
Morning glory. *See Ipomoea tricolor*, 77
Moss rose. *See Portulaca grandiflora*, 86
Mulches, 44–45
Myosotis sylvatica, 82

Nasturtium. *See Tropaeolum majus*, 92
Naturalizing annuals & wild-flowers, 34–35
Nemesia strumosa, 82
Nemophila, 83
Nicotiana, 83
Nierembergia, 83
Nigella damascena, 84

Ornamental pepper. *See Capsicum annuum*, 62

Painted-tongue. *See Salpiglossis sinuata*, 88
Pansy. *See Viola*, 93
Papaver, 84
Pelargonium, 84
Pentzia, 85
Pests, 50–51
Petunia hybrida, 85
Phlox drummondii, 86
Pinching, 48
Pincushion flower. *See Scabiosa atropurpurea*, 89
Pink. *See Dianthus*, 69
Planting locations
    choosing, 38
    edges & narrow spaces, annuals for, 27
    full sun, annuals for, 20–21
    hot & dry, annuals for, 23
    shady, annuals for, 22
Planting techniques
    from containers (transplants), 42–43
    from seed, 42, 43
Planting times, 38–39
Pocketbook plant. *See Calceolaria*, 60
Poor man's orchid. *See Schizanthus pinnatus*, 90
Poppy. *See Papaver*, 84
Portulaca grandiflora, 86
Pot marigold. *See Calendula officinalis*, 60
Powdery mildew, 51
Primrose. *See Primula*, 87
Primula, 87
Proboscidea louisianica, 87

Reseda odorata, 88
Rose-of-heaven. *See Lychnis coeli-rosa*, 80
Rudbeckia hirta, 88
Rust, 51

Safflower. *See Carthamus tinctorius*, 62
Sage. *See Salvia*, 88

Salpiglossis sinuata, 88
Salvia, 88
Sanvitalia procumbens, 89
Scabiosa atropurpurea, 89
Schizanthus pinnatus, 90
Seeds, growing annuals from, 42, 43
Senecio hybridus, 90
Shady gardens, annuals for, 22
Silk flower. *See Abelmoschus moschatus*, 54
Slipper flower. *See Calceolaria*, 60
Slugs, 51
Snails, 51
Snapdragon. *See Antirrhinum majus*, 57
Snow-on-the-mountain. *See Euphorbia marginata*, 71
Soils, 40–41
    acid & alkaline, 40
    preparation, 41
Spider flower. *See Cleome hasslerana*, 65
Staking, 48
Statice. *See Limonium sinuatum*, 79
Stock. *See Matthiola*, 81
Strawflower. *See Helichrysum bracteatum*, 75; *Helipterum roseum*, 76
Summer cypress. *See Kochia scoparia*, 78
Summer forget-me-not. *See Anchusa capensis*, 56
Summer poinsettia. *See Amaranthus*, 55
Sunflower. *See Helianthus annuus*, 74
Sunny locations, annuals for, 20–21, 23
Swan River daisy. *See Brachycome iberidifolia*, 58
Sweet alyssum. *See Lobularia maritima*, 80
Sweet pea. *See Lathyrus odoratus*, 78
Sweet scabious. *See Scabiosa atropurpurea*, 89
Sweet sultan. *See Centaurea*, 63

Tagetes, 90
Talinum paniculatum, 91
Texas pride. *See Phlox drummondii*, 86
Thunbergia alata, 91
Tithonia rotundifolia, 92
Toadflax. *See Linaria maroccana*, 79
Torenia fournieri, 92
Trachymene coerulea, 92
Transplanting, 42
Transplants, growing annuals from, 42
Transvaal daisy. *See Gerbera jamesonii*, 73
Treasure flower. *See Gazania rigens*, 72
Tree mallow. *See Lavatera trimestris*, 79
Tropaeolum majus, 92
Twinspur. *See Diascia barberae*, 70

Unicorn plant. *See Proboscidea louisianica*, 87

Velvet flower. *See Salpiglossis sinuata*, 88
Verbena hybrida, 93
Vervain. See *Verbena hybrida*, 93
Vinca rosea. *See Catharanthus roseus*, 62
Viola, 93

Wallflower. *See Cheiranthus cheiri*, 64
Warm-season annuals, 6
Watering, 44–45
Weeding, 48
Whiteflies, 51
White lace flower. *See Ammi majus*, 55
Wildflowers, 34
Winged everlasting. *See Ammobium alatum*, 56
Wishbone flower. *See Torenia fournieri*, 92

Zinnia elegans, 94